GUIDE TO WRITING
WEDDING SPEECHES
THE EASYWAY

ROLAND GARDNER

Easyway Guides

Easyway Guides

© Straightforward Publishing 2013

British Cataloguing in Publication data. A catalogue record is available for this book from the British Library.

9781847163301

Printed in the United Kingdom by Berforts Information press

Cover Design by Bookworks Islington

Contents

Introduction

Within the context of wedding planning as a whole, the formulation and delivery of wedding speeches by the various parties central to the wedding, such as the best man and groom, not to mention the father of the bride, play a small but very significant part in making sure that the big day goes well. Since the advent of the Civil Partnership Act 2004, which became law in 2005, civil partnerships are also now part of the civil ceremonies that take place outside of church weddings. Although this book refers to wedding speeches, the speeches can also be adapted to suit a civil partnership, or at least the essence of the speeches.

Whatever the venue, speeches will play an important part of the day and this brief book is intended to provide invaluable advice and guidance to all of those who will be involved in preparing and delivering a speech at a wedding or civil partnership.

Who says what in wedding speeches

Usually, the toastmaster and master of ceremonies will introduce the speeches at the end of the meal. The formal order of speakers is:

- Father of the bride (or a close family friend)

- The Groom

- The best man

If the bride, chief bridesmaid or guests want to speak, then they can do so. Although there is a recognised convention it is entirely up to the participants who does what and when. Traditionally, the speeches take place after the meal, but some couples decide to have them beforehand to allow the speakers to enjoy their meal free of nerves. below are some tips for each of the speakers on what to include in the speech.

Father of bride

The Father of the Bride speech should be personal and heart-warming and should sound uplifting about his daughter and son-in-law's future. Your speech should begin by thanking the guests for attending and should acknowledge the Groom's parents whilst welcoming your new son-in-law to the family.

When preparing your speech, think about what you want to say to your daughter; it may include your bond with her, special memories of her as a child and watching her grow in to the beautiful woman she is today. You can incorporate some funny anecdotes but be sure not to include anything that would embarrass her! If you know the Groom well, you can add a few stories of him too; however, he will get a lot of focus in the Best Man's speech so you can dedicate this time to your daughter.

You may want to talk about relationships and give some tips to the newly weds. Keep it light and avoid any pessimistic views from spoiling the occasion.

Groom

The Groom's wedding speech is made on behalf of himself and his Bride and uses the opportunity to personally thank the people involved in the wedding preparations. In his speech, he will toast the Bridesmaids and thank them for a job well done and will thank his groom's party for their support throughout. The Groom's speech should also include a special thank you to his parents and maybe even include some special memories with them.

Any family members or friends who could not attend the wedding should be remembered in the Groom's wedding speech.

As the Groom's speech comes before his Best Man's speech, he may wish to incorporate a few jokes and memories about his right hand man! Another entertaining and sentimental part of the Groom's speech is when he shares his first encounter with his wife and how his life has changed because of it!

Best man

The best man wedding speech is usually the most eagerly awaited of all the wedding speeches. Traditionally the best man speech is the last which gives the groom the chance to get one or two quick jokes in at the best man's expense. This can be a dangerous game as the best man can always have a couple of extra stories for his speech up his sleeve if he feels the need for revenge.

When preparing your best mans speech remember to think about your audience, find out the mix of people attending and try to weave something for everyone into your speech. Aim for your speech to be about 5 minutes but no more than 10 minutes. You will find that your best man speech takes longer when you deliver it on the day once all the laughter and cheering is factored in.

Bride

Nowadays more Brides are keen to say a few words on their special day. It is here you can thank your guests for coming and say a special thank you to your wedding entourage. Without your family and friends, your day wouldn't have been the same.

In your wedding speech you may want to acknowledge special friends and remember loved ones who aren't there with you on the day.

You can dedicate part of your Bride speech to thanking your parents for their support and for everything you have been through with them so far. You can include some special moments that you have shared with them that you hold dear to your heart and will cherish forever.

In your Bride speech you will want to say a special something to your new husband; maybe a special memory that you have when you first met, what was about him that made you fall in love with him and to tell him you are looking forward to the years ahead with him. Give him the recognition he deserves.

Maid of Honour/Best woman speeches

Speeches are not just for the men of the wedding party. Nowadays many ladies in the entourage like to say a few words and this is a great way to say a special thank you to the couple for asking you to play an important role on their special day.

The Maid of Honour speech should be light-hearted and have just the right amount of sentiment to allow for some oohs and aaahs! The guests will love to hear some funny stories about the bride; maybe some anecdotes of when you grew up together or a special milestone that you both shared. Try to include poignant message; say something from the heart. This is a great time for you to tell the Bride how much she means to you!

You can include in your Maid of Honour speech a special note about the Bride's parents and maybe a happy memory if you have a relationship with them.

In the Maid of Honour speech, you should thank the other Bridesmaids for their help in making today wonderful for their friends and for being a big part of the special day.

This book is divided into two halves, the first half being about the art and the craft of public speaking, how to formulate speeches and deliver those speeches, plus how to conquer nerves. I also cover the effective use of props when making a wedding speech.

The second half of the book concentrates on the actual writing of a speech and lays out two sample speeches per participant which will give invaluable guidance and help the person involved deliver a successful speech and make it a day to remember.

In addition to sample speeches, the final chapter outlines classic quotes, poems and jokes that can be used in wedding speeches. All in all, after reading this book you should be a good deal wiser, and happy in yourself that you will deliver a cracking good speech.

Good luck on the big day!

PART ONE

THE ART OF PUBLIC SPEAKING

1

PUBLIC SPEAKING AT WEDDINGS

Public speaking is very much an art and a skill that can be mastered by anyone. It is true to say that some people may be initially better equipped for the role of public speaker than others, by virtue of their own particular personality type. However, the truly effective public speaker learns the craft and applies certain techniques that generally derive from experience.

This book is primarily about delivering a speech at a wedding, and in the following chapters I will be alluding to the person who is not constantly engaged in addressing groups.

The person and the material

There are two vital ingredients in public speaking. The first is very much the person delivering the speech or other material to a group. The second is the nature of the material being delivered.

The Person

For some people, standing in front of an audience, whatever the size, is not a real problem. For others however, the very thought of exposing oneself to a group of people, and being so vulnerable, is a nightmare best avoided. When trying to put this into context it is important to remember that, when we communicate as part of a group, or simply on a one to-one basis with another, then we interact primarily through speech and body language. We are often confident within ourselves because we feel secure in that we are part of a group interacting and that all eyes are not on us alone, at least not for a protracted period. The situation is very different indeed when we are alone and faced with a group of people, strangers or not, and we have to present material. It means that we have to assume responsibility and take the lead and communicate successfully to others. Nervousness is very often the result when placed in this situation, because, until we can make contact with the audience and establish a rapport, we are very much alone and feel vulnerable.

Obviously, there are a number of factors influencing the levels of confidence and differences in attitude between people, such as the nature and type of the person and their background, their past experience, both within the family and in the world of work and numerous other experiences besides. All these will affect a persons ability to become an effective public speaker. Because that is what you will be, however briefly, at a wedding. A Public Speaker.

This publication cannot completely erase your nervousness. It cannot change your personality overnight. However, what it can certainly do is to raise your awareness to the root of that feeling in the context of public speaking and to help you become more confident. It can also show you that, whatever your personality type, you can become a successful public speaker by applying certain fundamental techniques.

Why do we feel nervous?

There are a number of reasons why we may feel nervous. You need to question yourself and ask yourself why. Was the sight of so many faces in front of you enough to frighten you and make you lose your self-confidence or are you plagued by the memory of previous mistakes? You need to remember that you change and develop as a person as you gain more experience and that past mistakes do not mean that you will repeat them.

Let's face it, most of us will experience nerves in a situation which is stressful to us. This is totally normal and quite often we become anxious and charged with adrenaline which drives us on. When it comes to speaking in public the adrenaline can be positive but excessive nerves are negative and can lead to aggression.

Fundamentally, the key to successful public speaking is the acquisition of confidence coupled with assertiveness which leads to the ability to effectively control a situation. If you are assertive and you know your subject matter you are likely to be confident and in control and less likely to feel nervous.

Be prepared!

Directly related to the above, preparation is everything and to feel confident with your material means that you are half way there already. Although I will be expanding on preparation a little later, there are a few fundamental tips that can help you along.

Before you present your speech at a wedding, you should listen to speakers, particularly good speakers as often as possible in order to gain tips. Notice the way that good and effective speakers construct their sentences. Listen for the eloquence. Remember, shorter sentences have a lot more impact and are easier to grasp than long sentences. They also act as a discipline for the speaker in that they will prevent him or her from straying off the point.

Another very important factor when approaching the day of your presentation is preparing yourself psychologically. Convince yourself that you are looking forward to the speech and that you will do well no matter what. Convey this to your audience as you open your presentation.

Finally, one of the main aids to effective public speaking is *experience* and that only comes through practice so it is essential that you take every opportunity offered you to sharpen your skills in this area.

In the next two chapters I will be concentrating on presentation and style. Fundamental to preparation as a speaker is the ability to relax and focus your mind and body on the task ahead.

Before you turn to chapter two, however, you should read the key points from chapter one overleaf.

KEY POINTS FROM CHAPTER ONE

- The truly effective public speaker learns the craft and applies certain techniques which generally derive from experience

- There are two vital ingredients in public speaking. The first is the person and the second is the material

- The key to successful public speaking is the acquisition of knowledge coupled with assertiveness which leads to the ability to control and direct a situation

- Listen to effective and successful speakers in order to gain tips

- Prepare yourself psychologically for your speech. Put yourself in a positive frame of mind!

2
PRESENTATION SKILLS-
HINTS ON STYLE

PERSONAL SKILLS

Body Language

People have a natural ability to use body language together with speech. Body language emphasizes speech and enables us to communicate more effectively with others. It is vitally important when preparing for the role of public speaker to understand the nature of your body language and also to connect this to another all- important element-*vision*.

Vision

People tend to take in a lot of information with their eyes and obviously presentations are greatly enhanced by use of visual aids. Together, when presenting to a group of people, as a public speaker, *body language and visual stimuli* are all important. A great amount of thought needs to go into the elements of what it is that you are about to present and the way you intend to convey your message. What you should not do, especially as a novice, is to stand up in front of a group and deliver a presentation off the top of your head. You need to carry out thorough research into what it is you are presenting and to whom you are presenting.

Developing a style

Every person engaged in public speaking will have his or her own style. At the one end of the spectrum there are those people who give no thought to what it is they are doing and have no real interest in the audience. For them it is a chore and one which should be gotten over as soon as is possible. Such public speakers can be slow, boring and ineffectual leaving only traces of annoyance in the audience's mind. Here, there is a definite absence of style.

At the other end of the spectrum are those who have given a great deal of thought to what they are doing, given a great deal of thought to their material and have a genuine interest in the audience. Such public speakers will be greatly stimulating and leave a lasting impression and actually convey something of some worth.

It does not matter what the occasion of your public speaking role is, wedding (best mans speech etc.) seminar, presentation to employers. The principles are the same-that is understanding your material, understand the nature of yourself as you relate to the material and how this will translate into spoken and body language and also how you will use visual aids to enhance the presentation.

Underlying all of this is your *own personal style*, partly which develops from an understanding of the above and partly from an understanding of yourself. Some presenters of material recognize their own speed of presentation, i.e. slow, medium or fast and also understand their own body language. Some are more fluent than others, use their hands more etc. Having recognized your own style what you need to do is to adjust your own way of presentation to the specific requirements of the occasion. The key point is to gain attention, get the message across and be stimulating to a degree. Obviously some occasions are more formal than others. You should study the nature of the occasion and give a lot of thought to what is required, i.e. degree of humor, seriousness etc. All of the above considerations begin to translate themselves into a style that you yourself will begin to recognize and feel comfortable with. Once this occurs you will find that, when presenting, your nerves will begin to melt away and your confidence begins to develop

Formal presentations

As this is a book about public speaking at weddings, with the emphasis on the more formal setting, we should now concentrate on the various elements that go to make up a successful presentation to a group.

There is not one particular style appropriate to public speaking. Each occasion will merit it's own approach. However, there are a few commonly observed rules.

Use of language

The use of language is a specific medium that must be understood when making a presentation. Obviously, if you are speaking publicly to a group of familiar people who know and understand you, a different approach will be needed and a different form of language, perhaps less formal, utilized than that used in front of a group who are totally unfamiliar. Nevertheless, using formal but simple language interspersed with funny remarks is undoubtedly one of the best ways to approach any form of audience, friends or not. You should certainly avoid too much detail and do not go overboard with funny comments as this will become tedious. Stick to the subject matter lightening up the occasion with a few anecdotes and witty comments. It is all about the right blend and pitch.

Body Language

We have briefly discussed body language. It is astounding how much you can tell about people in the street by simply observing their body language. Usually people form an impression about another within the first five minutes of meeting. It is essential, in a public speaking situation that your body language should reflect a confident personality with a good sense of humor. In order to achieve this you should think about the following:

Use of hands

- Use your hands to emphasize what you say and to invite the audience to accept your point
- Keep your hands open and keep your fingers open.
- Avoid putting your hands in your pocket and avoid closing them. Firmly avoid pointing fingers
- Co-ordinate your hand movements with your words.

Using facial expressions

People tend to concentrate on the face of a public speaker, in addition to the movements of the body. Obviously, your face, along with body language is a vehicle for expression. A smile every now and again is important. There are other actions that can help:

- Use of eyebrows for inviting people to accept your ideas

- Moving the head to look at all members of a group. Very important indeed to maintain a sense of involvement on the part of all

- Do not fix your eyes on one place or person for long. This will isolate the rest of the audience and may be interpreted as nervousness or a lack of confidence on your part

- Look at individuals every time you mention something in their area of expertise or are singling them out in a positive way

- Look at people even if they appear not to be looking at you

The face is a very important part of the communication apparatus and the use of this part of the body is of the utmost importance when public speaking.

Controlling your movements

In addition to the use of face and hands the way you move can have an effect on your audience. Your movements can vary from standing rigid and fixed to acting out roles and being fluid generally. There are in keeping with body language generally, certain rules relating to movement:

- Restrict your movements only to those that are most necessary. Avoid throwing yourself all over the place and distracting peoples attention from the emphasis of your presentation

- Always face the people that you are addressing. Never look at the floor or away from the audience, at least not for a prolonged period of time

Dress

When adopting the role of public speaker it is very important to be dressed in accordance with the standard of the occasion, or the nature of the occasion. Dressing formally does not mean automatically wearing a suit and tie. It does mean however that you should think in terms of power dressing. This means that you wish to make an impression on people, not just through what you say and do, not just through your body language or visual presentations but by the way you look.

People must be impressed. This means that you must give thought to what you wear, how you can help to achieve a sense of control through dress.

Attitude

Your attitude is crucial to your success in public speaking. Attitudes can be greatly influenced by nerves and by being ill-prepared. There is nothing worse than a public speaker who slowly degenerates into aggression or hostility through sarcasm or other forms of attack. Yet this is all too frequent. At all times you must maintain a professional and formal attitude that allows you to remain in control. You can think yourself into this state if you find yourself slipping or feel that you are losing control.

If you feel that you are straying in any way then you should get back on course. This can be achieved through a number of ways such as by changing the subject slightly in order to give yourself time to gather your wits or by asking the group to refocus on the subject in question.

Attitude is also disciplined by self-composure that can be engendered through relaxation which in turn is brought about by understanding the role of exercise and meditation, which we will be elaborating on a little later.

Formalities

Another fundamental rule of presentations is the way you open or introduce the presentation and the way you close. When public speaking, it is always necessary to introduce yourself even if most of the audience know who you are. It is vital that everyone knows who you are, who you represent, if anybody, and what you are there for. Having got these necessary formalities over with, the audience will feel more comfortable listening to you because they now have a point of reference.

Practicing presentations

Taking into account all of the above and then practicing. This is the absolute key to successful presentations and to effective public speaking. Practice most certainly lifts your confidence level up and assists you in staying in control The more time and effort that you spend practicing the less that you will have to worry about when presenting. Let's face it, a presentation is a live stage show. How do stand up comic's feel when they expose themselves to an audience? Develop a practicing technique by trying different methods:

- You should choose a topic that you are very interested in and prepare a short presentation on it.

- Stand in front of a mirror and present to yourself. Repeat this over and over observing different aspects of your style.

- Try to rectify any bad habits.

- Experiment with various styles and techniques until you find one that suits you.

- Try to film yourself if possible. Replay the film and observe yourself. This is one of the most effective ways of changing your style, or developing your style.

- Ask a friend to observe you and to make detailed criticism. Do not be afraid of criticism as this is always constructive

At this point you should be concentrating on style only. Do not worry about content as we will be discussing this a little later.

Now read the key points from chapter two.

KEY POINTS FROM CHAPTER TWO

- Body language emphasizes speech and helps us to communicate more effectively with others

- Visual stimuli is equally as important when public speaking

- It is very important to develop your own style as a public speaker

- The use of language is a specific medium which must be understood when public speaking

- Formal but simple language interspersed with funny remarks is one of the best ways to approach an audience

- The use of facial expressions is very important when addressing others

- The way you move can have a very important effect on an audience

- Your attitude is crucial to your success as a public speaker

- The way you open and close your presentation is of the utmost importance

- You should always practice presentations before the event

3

EFFECTIVE DELIVERY

In the last chapter, we discussed presentation and style. We also touched on delivery of a speech. In this chapter, we shall further concentrate on delivery.

Good delivery of a speech is a matter of being confident that you can remember what to say, and when and how you want to say it. It is also about communicating with an audience, not only through what you say, but through the attitude of your body, and by the expression of your voice. Good delivery, like a good speaking style, can be learned through adequate rehearsal and control of your nerves.

Presenting a speech

Most speakers in the context of a wedding decide to forego the security of relying on notes and rely instead on some form of memory jogging notes, or cue cards, to keep them on track. In this way, it is easier to communicate directly with the audience.

Some people have very good memories. If this is the case, you may decide to deliver the speech straight from the heart. Learning a script by heart means that the words are fixed in the brain. Because of this, the speaker will usually find it very difficult to move away from the pattern and introduce new phrases or anecdotes.

You should watch people who are reciting from memory. Their energy and attention is, usually, turned inwards instead of concentrating on the audience. If you are trying to remember what is coming next, you are not going to be able to direct your energies towards the audience. The only people who are really capable of delivering a memorized speech to an audience are trained actors who have had many years experience.

Posture and movement

One of the main elements of your appearance that your audience will detect at first sight is that of your posture, the way you move. As with many animals, your posture and movement will send strong signals about you as a person and also about your attitude to the people you are with. For example, stooping and bowing your head indicates uncertainty and that we are unsure of our ground. Holding the head up high indicates confidence and security.

From the moment you face your audience, make sure you pay attention to your posture. Hold your shoulders square, head high and avoid slouching. Sit towards the front of a chair, rather than sitting back. Do not cross your legs at the knee. Try to convey the impression that you are relaxed but alert.

When you talk, do so with purpose. Always speak on your feet and fix your eyes on the audience. Stand upright, do not slouch. Place your feet a few inches apart with the weight on the balls rather than on the heels of the feet. This means that your body is balanced and that you are leaning towards the audience slightly. From this basic speaking position, you should be able to move in a relaxed yet purposeful manner. Avoid shuffling around.

Eye contact

It would be useful to watch an actor when they are making eye contact and to try to work out what it is they are doing with their eyes. In most cases, the actor is doing his or her level best to avoid looking into the eyes of another person.

By making eye contact, we are expressing our openness towards other people. We are also showing that we are not frightened of them and that we are interested in their feelings, thoughts and reactions. When the contact is made, a direct line of communication is opened up and the listener's attention is held. Making eye contact with an audience is one of the most valuable skills that a speaker can learn. Eye contact can be practiced in almost any social situation, and you will be surprised how it changes people's reaction to you. They will become more attentive and more willing to trust what it is you have to say. They will begin to look upon you as a more approachable person-exactly the kind of response that you want from your audience.

When you are speaking to a group, avoid picking out one single member of the audience and making eye contact exclusively with him or her. This will make that person very uncomfortable and the rest of the audience will begin to feel excluded. Make eye contact with different individuals round the room so that you take in the whole audience.

If you are inexperienced and nervous, you may not wish to make eye contact straight away. In this case, deliver your first couple of lines to a point above the audience's head. However, as soon as the time is appropriate, start making eye contact. This should come as you feel more confident.

You will find that if you have opted to read your speech from a script, you will find it very difficult to make time to make eye contact. Eye contact is central to delivering your message in a personal and effective way and, for this reason, it is important to free your eyes from the written word.

If you cannot perfect the art of making eye contact with your audience then you will probably find that your speech-making efforts are doomed to failure.

Hand gestures

As with body movement, hand gestures can add to, rather than detract from, the spoken word. They should be produced as part of your enthusiasm for and knowledge of your subject.

You should watch how others use gestures in everyday conversations, such as pointing, stabbing, clenching the fist and so on. There are two things to avoid when it comes to hand gestures. First, beware of fidgeting, this can be irritating. Second, try not to make too many meaningless gestures as these may confuse the audience. Do not, for example, keep waving your arms around for emphasis.

Facial expression

The golden rule on facial expression is: smile, but not too much. A smile means that you are friendly, are happy to be there and are relaxed. However, try not too smile fixedly through thick and thin, allowing no other response to register on your face. People will mistrust you and see you as behaving unnaturally.

Voice control

The third element in delivering a speech is your voice. Good vocal delivery can be broken down into two factors: volume-speaking to be heard; expression-speaking to be understood. The basic skill in voice control is breathing.

Expression

The way a speaker expresses his or her words adds to their meaning in much the same way as hand gestures. Expression involves three elements: pitch variation-the tone of your voice; pace-the speed at which you speak; and phrasing-sculpting your phrases into a meaningful form. Rehearsal with a tape recorder should enable you to pinpoint faults in your expression.

Pitch

As a rule, younger people tend to have higher pitched voices than older people. It follows that, because older people are considered to have more authority than younger people, those with lower voices are thought of in the same way. Emotional state can also determine pitch, nervousness being characterized by higher pitch for example.

Some teachers of public speaking advocate that you work towards a lower tone for these reasons. However, if one of the keys to good delivery is being natural then this may not be a good idea. For the majority of people, controlled breathing and careful phrasing should automatically improve the tone of voice.

Pace

It is important to ensure that the pace of your speech is measured. You must give your audience time to hear and assimilate the words you are saying, and yourself time to think where the next sentence is coming from. Slower than normal speech also indicates that you have something important to say.

As you work with your speech, add indications of pauses of different lengths. These will help you to add emphasis. Slowing speech can also give you time to improve your diction.

Phrasing

The words you have written out in a full script fall into small groups-perhaps sentences or parts of sentences (individual clauses). To better communicate the meaning of each of these groups of words, you need to take each one as an individual unit and try to imbue it with the single meaning that it contains.

Different meanings require different 'shapes'. A question, for example, should be spoken with an upturn at the end. Without the upturn, the question could be taken as a statement.

Using a microphone

In general, try to avoid using a microphone-it can make the voice sound unnatural and hinders the task of appearing to be conversational. It may, however, be unavoidable in certain circumstances to use a microphone, such as in the open air and so on. You should always check with the organizers of the event whether they expect you to use a microphone. Try the microphone out and make sure that all can hear you, particularly those at the rear. If you have to use a microphone, it is best to practice, probably at home. You must get your voice to the right volume and you must find out how far away from the microphone you can move before your voice gets lost. Teach yourself to avoid feedback at all costs as this can severely distract the audience.

Presenting visual aids

You might have incorporated any form of visual aid into your presentation. By using props, music or slides in your presentation, you will underline everything that you say with a big impact. Your speech will be funnier, punchier and the more memorable for it. Props are a great way to break the ice at the beginning of a speech, a great way to ease the tension that everyone feels at the start of a speech.

The following are two useful props:

Slide show
Slides are easy to set up and can be put to great effect. Pick up to ten photos to tell a story. All eyes will be on the photos and not on you.
Musical history
Make a montage of around 20 photos, covering your subjects childhood, adolescence, holidays and so on. You could maybe add a piece of music to accompany them. In this way, the audience will be totally absorbed.

Anything else you can think of, such as a piece of clothing from your subjects punk past or any memento will usually go down well. Be creative in the use of props and you can greatly enhance your speech.

Time for rehearsal

Skilful use of equipment such as microphones and visual aids can be learned through practice and familiarity. In the same way, all the techniques that combine to make a good delivery-effective use of notes, understanding and controlling the body and voice-can be assimilated through rehearsal until they are second nature. It is therefore essential, especially if speaking in public is a new experience, that you devote some time to rehearsing. Depending on your schedule, you may have a little or a lot of time to rehearse. Rehearsals need not take a long time, possibly an hour or so every session, depending on the length of the speech. You should allow enough time before the actual speech to fit enough practice sessions in.

What to look for in rehearsal

There are several stages in a progressive rehearsal of a speech. You may begin with the full script of the speech in front of you, or notes, and you may intend to simply read from the script on the day or to produce it as notes. Here are some suggestions what to look out for at each stage. Whatever stage you are at, it is always a good idea to stand up and try to deliver the speech to an imaginary audience. It is also a good idea to rehearse with your visual aids right from the start.

1. At the first stage, you are either working from notes or from an annotated script. Read through. Try out alternative phrases and descriptions, add pauses, and try to decide

whether your speech hangs together as a logical and coherent train of thought. Note down any changes, and try the whole thing again. It may take a number of read-throughs before you are happy with your speech.

Ask yourself these questions:

- Is this speech about the topic that I have chosen?
- Is there anything superfluous that I can cut out?
- Is this speech appropriate to the audience and the occasion?
- Am I using the right visuals for the right reasons?
- Is this speech likely to help me achieve my objectives?

Time your speech. Make sure that it is shorter than the time limit you have been given-you need to leave time for audience reaction. Make any cuts necessary to ensure that you do not run over time. If you run short, you can always fill in by taking questions. However, do not run over, this is not acceptable.

When you are certain that the material and the basic form of your speech are right, transfer it to cue cards, or whichever form of notes that you have chosen. If you are already working from notes, it would be a good idea to rewrite them, to take account of the changes that you have made. If you intend to work from the script, it might be a good idea to rewrite it.

2. From this point on, try not to add anything to your notes or script. Run through the speech a couple of times more. If you have picked out a couple of sentences that you would like to learn by heart, do it now. Keep experimenting with new words and phrases. Work hard to draw out each thought into a full picture of what you mean to say. Vary the pitch, pace

and volume of your voice. If it helps, you should rehearse in a quiet room Away from distractions.

3. At this stage, you might like to record your speech, so that you can analyze the oral element of your delivery. Do not play back straight away, leave it an hour or so then you will come to it with a fresh mind. Listen hard and ask yourself the following questions:

- Are you speaking slowly enough?
- Are you varying the pace slightly?
- Are you making good use of pauses?
- Do your sentences turn down at the ends?
- Are you giving the right kinds of expression to your words?
- Are there places where you are having difficulty expressing yourself?
- Do you use fillers: er, um, you know, you see and so on?

Check the timing again-it is very easy to over elaborate once you are familiar with your material.

4. Next, draft in a friend who is able to take in the whole experience of your delivery-your appearance and message as well as your voice. Ask him or her to be objective and constructive in their criticisms. As you deliver your speech again, imagine that your friend is in the middle of a whole group of people and practice making eye contact with the audience.

Ensure that no punches are pulled in this encounter with your friend as it is vital that you finally polish up your speech and your method of delivery. Remember, at this stage, the time is drawing close for you to stand up and present your speech. It must be as perfect as possible before the day.

Now read the key points from chapter 3

KEY POINTS FROM CHAPTER THREE

- Good delivery of a speech is a matter of being confident that you can remember what to say, and when and how you want to say it.

- Most speakers forego the security of notes and use cue cards as an aid to effective delivery.

- The most effective method of delivering a script of almost any kind is to abbreviate the script to a series of key words.

- Whichever way you decide to deliver a speech, ensure that you have practiced thoroughly.

- The style of your dress will mark you out and people will categorize you on the spot.

- Audiences will pick up on the way that you move.

- Audiences will also pick up on eye contact, hand gestures and facial expressions.

- Control of the voice is very important when delivering a speech.

- Adequate rehearsals are very important indeed before delivering a speech.

4

DEALING WITH NERVES

We discussed public speaking and nervousness at the beginning of this book. However, now that the big day has approached, you may be feeling more nervous than ever. Therefore, it is necessary to look at nerves in more detail.

Fear need not become an obstacle to your success as a speaker. In fact, nervousness can become a positive aid to your ability to put across your message, as long as you learn to take control of it.

Perseverance in the face of fear

In moments of panic it might be difficult to remember why it ever occurred to you to speak in public. Remember, you have been invited to the wedding, you volunteered and now the big day has arrived.

Fear of public speaking

The best way to describe how a person feels when they are frightened is to list a number of symptoms: sweating, blushing, racing pulse, clumsiness or shaking limbs and a blank mind. The key to fighting debilitating fear is to think beyond the symptoms to the cause.

When asked to list reasons why they may feel fear when faced with speaking in public, the following are often listed as reasons:

- I am inexperienced
- I do not know enough about the subject.
- I am afraid of the audience.
- My mind may go blank.
- The equipment may go wrong.
- I may make a complete fool of myself by saying or doing something stupid.

All of these worries are founded on one fear: the fear of the unknown.

As a novice speaker, making your debut, you may consider yourself in a particularly frightening situation. However, every speaker you have ever heard once made a maiden speech. The fear of the novice quickly disintegrates as soon as that maiden speech is over, so you might as well take the bull by the horns and do it now.

What else is there in the speaking situation that is unknown, and therefore to be feared? You may feel that you may lose your thread half way through or that your mind will go blank. It is in your power to get rid of this fear by thorough preparation. If you are not sure of your subject, take action to change it. You may be able to do this by narrowing the field by covering only those subjects of which you are certain. If you think that you might lose your way, take time to rehearse well in advance, so that you can extemporize with ease. Extemporization is merely elaborating a theme. If you know your subject well enough, if you have planned your speech logically, and if you have made good memory jogging notes, you should have no fear of not finding your way back to the right path should you stray for a moment.

Remember, you are the one in charge, you are the one who has control and will deliver a speech that others will enjoy and remember. This is the attitude that you should have, not over confident but just right-at ease and relaxed, comfortable with yourself, and in command of your subject matter.

Relate the art of public speaking to that of an everyday conversation. Very rarely do you lose control of an everyday conversation. There is no reason why you should think any differently of public speaking.

Practical ways of controlling fear

Fear is merely the product of lack of preparation. However, fear is not a rational sentiment, it is a physical response and, try as you might, you cannot banish it. An alternative way of tackling anxiety is through the body, rather than through the brain. People are more prone to anxiety in certain circumstances, and if you can avoid those circumstances then it is possible to reduce stress significantly.

General health

Because fear is a physical reaction, people often find that, when they are feeling below par, they become anxious about trivial things. In the days before your speech, rest and eat properly and keep off alcohol. Take a couple of brisk walks.

Try to avoid stimulants such as caffeine, cigarettes, etc. Try to relax naturally and learn a good breathing exercise.

In seeking to reduce your anxiety, it is not necessary to eradicate it altogether. A taste of nerves keeps your mind alert. It is important to stay on your mettle if you are to appear at your best.

Most of all-remember that you have very little to lose and a lot to gain by speaking in public.

5

DELIVERING YOUR PRESENTATION

On the day

All of your preparation has been leading towards one particular day, that of the event in which you are to speak, in this case a wedding. The following advice is aimed at reducing the possibility that something might go wrong, and at giving you the chance to control your nerves and perform to the best of your ability.

You are at the point where your speech has been (or should have been!) written and your visual and other aids if appropriate have been prepared. You have also acquired knowledge about the setting. If possible, you should allow yourself time for a dress rehearsal prior to delivering your speech.

Of course, a dress rehearsal may not be necessary on all occasions. However, if you are speaking in front of a lot of people then you may want to at least spend some time taking in the area you will speak in and also to run through a few motions. At the same time, put some thought into what you are going to wear. Preparing clothes the night before will lead to trouble. At the same time, ensure that your car is reliable enough to get you to the event or that you know what the public transport arrangements are.

On the eve

Apart from the moments when you arise from your feet to speak, the evening before can be the most stressful time as you anticipate the possible horrors of the following day.

Many people leave their final checks till the day of the speech. It is a good idea to use the evening before to check your speech, equipment and clothes and to get a good night's sleep.

Many people also try to allay the night-before fears by shutting themselves away and practicing their speech over and over again. Practice once and put the speech out of your mind. If you keep practicing at this late stage you will only increase your nerves.

The eve of the speech is also a good time to check all your visual aids and props, if you are going to use any. Make sure that all the equipment is working and that you have all the material that you require.

Take time to lay out your clothes for the occasion, checking all the fine details, such as buttons, shoes cleaned and so on. Take time out to relax, simply resting and focusing your mind for the next day.

Make sure that you leave adequate time to set out and before you leave, check that you have everything that you need:

- Your speech-cue cards or crib sheet or script.
- Your spectacles if appropriate.
- A notebook containing the contact number should you get lost or delayed, and also details of the travel arrangements.
- A pen or pencil.

- Some tissues.
- Small change for telephone calls or parking charges.

Checking out the venue

At the earliest possible opportunity, pay a visit to the room in which you will be speaking. Ensure that the layout is adequate and that all the equipment needed is there. Contact the organizers if there are any discrepancies.

Check that the air condition is suitable. If the room feels too hot or cold, make sure that the air conditioning, if any, is adjusted. Listen for audible distractions, such as a bar or kitchen, so that you can prepare for them when you make your speech.

Microphones

For rooms and smaller venues the natural voice can be used. However, for larger halls a microphone is essential. When you are using a microphone keep your head about four inches away when you speak. Avoid any feedback or handling noise.

Appearance

As we mentioned earlier aim at being comfortable and smart.

For the woman

Keep the hair away from the face, so that it is not masked, but retain a soft style. Earrings can soften the face and add interest, but avoid the large dangling variety; they will be a distraction; a colorful scarf or brooch adds a touch of sophistication and interest to the neckline; avoid wearing dull colors unless they are offset by something bright and cheerful; check that your hemlines are straight especially if wearing a full skirt.

For the man

Wear a well fitting suit and shirt with the cuffs just showing below the jacket. The tie should be neatly tied; black shoes are preferable to brown; brown tends to distract the eye. Colored dark socks should be worn, rather than white. Make sure that the socks cover the calves adequately; you should smile as often as possible because this gives the impression of being confident.

Being sociable

When you are satisfied that all the on-the-spot arrangements are complete, you may have time to socialize. You may be asked to join your hosts or gathering members of the audience for a drink. This is a very useful time.

If members of the audience see that you are mingling with them in an affable sort of way, you will reinforce the feeling that you are friendly and relaxed and also sympathetic, someone who takes an interest. It will also enable you to judge the mood of the audience and take your mind off your speech.

Moments before your speech

A few minutes before you are due to speak, begin to prepare yourself. Now is the time to make that final trip to the lavatory or to take a final brisk walk to freshen yourself up. If you have to sit through other peoples speeches be alert and interested. You will probably be just as visible as the person speaking and you must do nothing to distract the audiences attention.

You may also wish to edit your speech in the light of something that has been said. Keep an eye on the time. If the other speaker goes on too long then you may need to edit your speech accordingly.

Standing up to make your speech

Make a good first impression. This will work wonders for your confidence. If you are walking up to a platform, adopt an easy gait with your arms swinging naturally and your body straight. It is more likely that, because the occasion is a wedding you will be standing up at a table.

When you are being introduced, look at the introducer and keep an open and alert face. When the introduction is over, take a deep breath, face the audience and begin. Smile and relax.

Show your audience that you are happy to be there, by being warm and relaxed. Animate your body movements. Positive body language is very important. If you are using a lectern, place your notes on it with a quick glance down, and then look at your audience. Smile as you make your opening remarks. This way you appear much more approachable and attractive.

Focus on your audience. When there is a large audience present, it is sometimes difficult to know where to look when making a speech. If there is strong stage lighting, it is unlikely that you will be able to see your audience, in which case individual eye contact is impossible.

If there is a central exit light at the back of the hall, use that as your main focus point. In between times, the eye can travel to the right hand side of the hall and then the left, always homing back to the exit sign. This gives the illusion of looking at the audience.

And then begin your speech!

The end

It's all over! You've done it, you have made a cracking speech and everyone is happy. This is time to take stock and consider the whole process, learning from your mistakes and congratulating yourself on your success.

Don't forget, you have done what you set out to do-that is deliver a speech in public. The author hopes that the advice and information contained within this book has helped that process.

Now read the key points from chapter 5 overleaf.

KEY POINTS FROM CHAPTER FIVE

- All the initial preparations have been for the actual presentation

- Check lighting, microphones and give thought to how you present

- Avoid irritating mannerisms

- Have regard for your appearance

- Your entrance is all important-make a good first impression

- Remember all that you have read and take control

6

WRITING A WEDDING SPEECH

Researching the speech

The first thing anyone should do when contemplating how to write a wedding speech is to grab a notepad and pen and write down anything and everything they know about the subject and subject matter. In fact, wherever you go, keep a notebook handy for making on the spot notes - you will be surprised as to where and when you will find inspiration and thoughts.

Once you've done your research, the next stage is to add your own unique ideas and material to the mix. For those looking for a unique angle to approach the speech from, you could try one of the five following suggestions:

Talk about similarities between the Bride and Groom and famous people they share their birthday with or a modern day celebrity couple they 'are most like'. Alternatively, relate the Bride, Groom or both to current affairs or celebrity gossip.

Find out what astrological traits the Bride and/or Groom should have, what their forenames & surnames mean or 'what happened on this day in history' and apply them accordingly.

Develop a Top 5 list on whatever subject you fancy – 'The Top 5 reasons I got married today', 'The Top 5 reasons my wife and I will miss our daughter', 'The Top 5 reasons why the Bride doesn't know what she's let herself in for' etc. Make it relevant, short and a mix of sincerity and humour, and you can't go wrong. This is also an ideal intro as all you are doing is simply reading from a sheet of paper David Letterman style.

Use a theme for your speech. If the couple are footy mad fans weave in as many football team names into the speech, or for sweet-toothed lovers, mention as many chocolate bars as you can and see how many the guests can spot!

Writing the speech

There's no magic formula you can apply to the physical writing of a wedding speech, no universal set of rules that apply to all, it's simply a matter of trial and error. For some, armed with all the research and material it will literally be a five minute job, for others it could take weeks. But regardless of which camp you fall into, the following hints and tips should help everyone wanting to know how to write a wedding speech.

- Make sure your speech has a definite beginning a structured middle bit and a big finish.

- Write the speech on a computer, ideally using a password-protected word processing programme to keep it away from prying eyes and make it easily editable. If you hand-write your speech, keep it under lock and key and take photocopies just in case.

- Be natural in your writing style and avoid words that you wouldn't normally use.

- Remember that your speech is heard not read, so make sure the language isn't too formal or impersonal. If in any doubt, run your speech past a trusted source for their opinion.

- Don't expect to write a speech that even Martin Luther King or JFK would be proud of with your first effort. Write, re-write and refine your speech over time until you are happy with the result. Don't be afraid to reword any parts of the speech which you struggle to remember or read out.

7

Sample Wedding Speeches and Toasts

Having now covered the art of presentation in depth, it is now time to look at sample speeches that cover the range of speeches that will be covered at a wedding reception. The following speeches will be covered in this order, which is the traditional order at the reception:

Father of the bride
Bridegroom
Best Man
Bride
Maid of Honour

Father of the Bride or brother/sister or friend of the family.

The opening speech by either the father of the bride, or in his absence a member of the family or a friend should contain within it:

- Thanks to the guests for coming and participating in the special day

- Thanks to everyone who as contributed to the cost of the wedding

- Compliments and praise to the bride and welcome to her new husband and family

- A toast to the bride and the groom

The first speech below represents a typical speech delivered by the father of the bride.

Father of the bride-Example 1

A very good afternoon ladies and gentlemen. I'm David and I have the undoubted honour of being the father of this blushing bride. However, I'm fully aware that my main function this afternoon is to warm you up, the audience, for the star performers who will speak later.

Most of you will know of Emma's interest in fashion so I thought I would try to make my speech like that well known item of fashion clothing, the mini skirt - short enough to be interesting and long enough to cover the essentials.

Today is, of course, a celebration, but not just of the love that has united Emma and Phillip in their marriage today, but also of the families that have created, moulded and influenced the lives of these two special people. So my wife Sheila and I would like to extend a very warm welcome to Phillips parents Lorraine and Arthur and to relatives and friends of both families.

A special welcome also to those who have travelled some way to be with us today. We have people from Portsmouth, Nottingham, London and Birmingham.

Thank you all for joining us in celebrating this very special day.

Looking back, I clearly remember another very special day for Sheila and I, on a Sunday just 10,302 days ago when I witnessed the birth of our first child, Emma. Well, that seems like only yesterday. I have many memories of her as a baby. I've seen her wet herself and crawl around on the floor but I think that's enough about her 18th birthday.

There have been many memorable days along the way. Emma having acute appendicitis in France on, little did we know at the time, Phillip's birthday, in 1991. This will never be forgotten.

Her sleep walks are legendary - two stand out in particular. The first was the time she woke Sheila at 3 am to get her to come to Emma's room to sort out the mouse that was in there. Chris stayed and talked to her only to realise after a while that Emma was asleep. Then there was the time she woke us up to say that burglars had telephoned to say that they were about to break-in - again whilst she was asleep!

But warmer memories are plentiful such as -

-her wearing a hat for all of the three weeks we holidayed in America in 2000;
-the time she chose to sit down in Lake Cosenostra,
-her playing against Wolverhampton Wanderers - the ladies team,
-completing a half marathon, and, of course,
-her degree success in 2007.

As I accompanied Emma here today there could not have been a prouder man and as we walked side by side I thought, and I'm sure you'll agree, that Jodie looked absolutely stunning ... and Phillip, well he looked absolutely stunned!

Of course, fathers are naturally biased where daughters are concerned, but in Emma I see an independent, intelligent, beautiful young woman, a daughter to be truly proud of. A daughter who, throughout her life, has always been ready to face a challenge. Some would say, however, that she's about to face her biggest challenge of all...which brings me to the other half of this partnership.

Seriously, when his child is young, a father sometimes contemplates the image of the man his daughter will marry. Will he be kind - intelligent - thoughtful - generous?

Just over 5 years ago Emma introduced us to a young man with DREADLOCKS - .Phillip.

We are delighted that Emma now has a husband with all these attributes and more.

During the time we've known Phillip we've come to realise how much he means to Emma. When you see how gorgeous Emma looks today, it proves the one thing I've always known about Phillip – he is clearly a man of vision...Occasionally blurred, sometimes double, but nonetheless a man of vision - and they have been fortunate to have found each other. So it's a pleasure, Phillip, to formally welcome you into our family.

I was struck by his thoughtfulness in the course of a conversation we had one Monday after work in The Bay Horse in June last year. Phillip asked for my permission to propose to Emma. He had clearly given the matter a great deal of thought and Emma was at the centre of everything he said.

An example of that generosity I mentioned just now was shown last November when Phillip treated me to day out. A trip to Twickenham to see the Barbarians play Australia - alas we, well most of us in the room, lost 11 - 60. To return the favour I treated Allun to an afternoon at The Mem to watch Bristol Rovers play Bradford City - somehow we won 2 - 1. I probably got the better of that exchange but Phillip's done very well today, hasn't he?

And perhaps the ultimate compliment comes from Emma's brothers Roger and Robert who think he's sound.
Now, it's customary on these occasions for me to offer the happy couple some worldly advice on marriage. As is the fashion today, Emma and Phillip have already set up home together and so already know a lot about each other. I am delighted that both are making very good progress in their chosen careers yet also find time to do lots together, for example the surprise birthday treat a day trip to The Peak District and holidays to Tenerife, Morocco and Canada.

So Phillip, remember there is no challenge in a marriage that can't be overcome by one or more of the following:

Ok, I was wrong, Ok, You were right, Yes Dear And the most important - OK love! Just buy it!

From recent personal experience I would say don't make assumptions, for example - Sheila was enjoying a glass of wine one fine summer's evening on the patio with me. I heard her say, 'I love you so much. I don't think I could ever live without you'. Wow, I thought and asked Sheila, 'Is that you or the wine talking?'. She replied, 'It's me...talking to the wine'.

Finally, there is a saying, which goes something like 'Happy marriages begin when we marry the ones we love, and they blossom when we love the ones we marry.' So, Emma and Phillip may your marriage be a truly happy one, may it begin with an unforgettable honeymoon in America and may you both have a long and wonderful life together.

Ladies and gentlemen would you please be upstanding and raise your glasses for the toast - The Bride and Groom.

The Father of the Bride Wedding Toast

The Father of the Bride will be the first of the speechmakers to raise a wedding toast.

At the end of his speech, he will lift up his glass, say a few words then raise a toast the Bride and Groom. It is traditional for his wedding toast to include sentiments of a healthy and happy life for the newlyweds, although there are no restrictions whatsoever on what else the Father of the Bride has to say.

The following is a short example of a typical Father of the Bride wedding toast:

"Now I invite you all to raise a toast to my beautiful daughter and my son-in-law. May they live a wonderfully healthy life together and enjoy many, many years of happiness.
To the Bride and Groom."

Brother of the bride-Example speech

The speech below represents a typical speech by the brother of the bride, but can be adapted for any member of the family.

I would like to start by saying, on behalf of my Mum, Grace and myself, what a real pleasure it is to welcome Stephen's family, our family, friends and everyone in between that that join us here in celebrating Sophie and Stephen's special day. I know that many of you have travelled a long way to be here.

I'd like to say a particular thank you to my Aunty Alice who has a phobia of car journeys and would have needed to be sedated to make it down from Yorkshire. I'm glad to see you made it and that they managed to bring you round in time for the ceremony!

I'd also like to say thank you for everyone involved in making today special – I know that over the past year Sophie and Stephen have put in a huge amount of planning and effort to make today a relaxed and laid back celebration and I am sure you will all agree it has been an incredible day so far.

It seems that even the weather has been planned to ensure the perfect day.

Although this a joyous occasion, I can't let this moment pass without saying we all know we would all rather have our Dad up here today giving this speech. I know that if were still with us he couldn't be any more proud of Sophie than me and Mum are right now at the fantastic person she has grown up to be. I know too that he would have been delighted in the prospect of having Stephen as his Son in Law.

As I have the pleasure of being the first of the speeches I get to be the first to officially congratulate the happy couple and to tell

Sophie how very beautiful I think she looks today. I don't want people to think I am showing favouritism. – Stephen…you look magnificent too!!

As Sophie's brother, it has been a true privilege to be able to walk my sister down the isle today and watch her exchange vows at Codsall church. The church has a lot of memories for the **** family and it was fitting for it to be the starting point for such a new happy chapter in our family history.

Standing up here now looking at Sophie I can hardly believe that she's my baby sister! There are nearly 10 years between us and I always wondered if she was a happy accidental addition to the family – Well as it turns out Sophie had been planned all along and it was me that was the unexpected one!!

It is fitting at times like this to think back on notable moments in my sisters life that have impacted on me.

My sister has never been one to crave the centre of attention but when she does she does it in style. As a small child she decided to wander off in her green quilted romper suit for a walk on her own. Not until half the village had been drafted in to look for her and we were all beginning to panic did she decide to toddle back home as if nothing had happened!

Stephen, you will be pleased to know that she has not continued this Houdini act into adult life!

There is also an episode in her early years regarding chocolate buttons that Sophie has asked me not to mention. On account of the fact that she has far more embarrassing stories about me I will honour that wish – but I'm sure if you buy her a glass of champagne later she'd be potty not to tell you! I have it on good authority that Stephen still has a packet of buttons tucked away for those difficult occasions!

It seems only yesterday that I was driving Sophie to primary school in my first car - a rusting 1975 Triumph with tasteful red vinyl seats. Hard to believe now that my tall sis used to need a cushion to see out the window and to stop her from slipping off the seat! She used to love those journeys listening to my rather dodgy collection of 80's tapes which is why to this day she has a love of Spandua Ballet that isn't normal for a 28 year old!

Growing up with an older brother clearly has had an effect over the years as my sister is fully aware of the plot of Star Wars and has a love of action movies over romantic comedies – a fact that I think Stephen should thank me for on a daily basis.

I have to say that she wasn't a tom boy though as she also had My Little Pony collection large enough to open a stables with and was a huge fan of Boy George with a life sized poster adorning her bedroom wall! I would like to stress for the record that neither of these traits were anything to do with my influence!

In later life Sophie successfully went to University and got a 2:1 in her degree – another proud moment in the **** family – even if it did mean she beat my grades!

Sophie wasn't all that keen I remember to give up the life of the student but I managed to coax her into the world of work by applying for a job at **** – or the family firm as we liked to think of it as both Dad and I had worked there over the years!

I am pleased to say that she has not only found a job she enjoys but also a husband which I think you will all agree is not a bad days work!!

For those of you that know Sophie well you will know she's a keen lover of animals and misses being surrounded by pets as she was growing up - even now I know she'd get a puppy tomorrow if the room could be found at home.

Well Sophie – you now have a Steven instead - who thinking about it has many of the characteristics of a puppy – full of enthusiasm, always playful and friendly and always wins over everyone they meet. I just hope he also doesn't chew the furniture or wee on the carpet!!

Not having Dad around has made us a close family and it is a real pleasure to welcome Steven into the fold – Having been outnumbered by both my Mum and Sophie over the years I'm grateful at last for the additional male support!

When I first got to know Stephen it was when we worked together long before he met my sister. I remember one particular day we had a meeting in Norwich which involved a 6 hour round trip and seemed to involve a lot of talk about mountain biking. A subject I knew nothing about at the start of the journey but by the end I felt I was qualified to downhill Ben Nevis! I thought back then he was a good guy, little did I know then that one day he would become my Brother in Law. I seem to remember I got us a McDonalds burger on the way back. If I'd known one day you were going to take my sister off my hands I'd have got you the fries and drink as well!

Joking aside, Steven is one of the most genuine and considerate people I have met and I can honestly say I have never known Sophie to be happier than in the time they have been together.

It is clear to me as to everyone that knows them that they are soul mates that compliment each other perfectly and as cheesy as it sounds I couldn't have asked for a better man to marry my sister.

It is traditional on these occasions to end by giving some advice to the married couple. I can't draw on the experiences of my own illustrious married life.. just yet but I have unearthed a few words of wisdom on this complex subject.

To Sophie,

If you want something from Stephen, ask for it. Remember, Stephen is a man, hints do not work!

To Stephen,

I'm going to borrow the words of Oscar Wilde, "Women are meant to be loved, not understood."

Marriage will bring you many things, loyalty, self restraint, obedience and a whole host of other virtues you wouldn't have needed had you stayed single.

And most useful piece of advice I can give to you to maintain a long and happy marriage - always remember to put the loo seat down after you!

On a slightly less irreverent note…to you both…

Marriage in this day and age is far from easy - With all the external pressures of day-to-day life - you will need to grow together in mutual trust and understanding - whilst not losing sight of what first brought you together - In other words - may your love be modern enough to survive the times - yet old-fashioned enough to last forever.

And so finally....it's my very great pleasure.... to propose the toast to the happy couple. Ladies and Gentlemen ...will you please be upstanding ....and raise your glasses............. to the Bride and Groom.

****

Bridegrooms speech

The Groom's wedding speech is made on behalf of himself and his Bride and uses the opportunity to personally thank the people involved in the wedding preparations. In his speech, he will toast the Bridesmaids and thank them for a job well done and will thank his groom's party for their support throughout. The Groom's speech should also include a special thank you to his parents and maybe even include some special memories with them.

Any family members or friends who could not attend the wedding should be remembered in the Groom's wedding speech.

As the Groom's speech comes before his Best Man's speech, he may wish to incorporate a few jokes and memories about his right hand man! Another entertaining and sentimental part of the Groom's speech is when he shares his first encounter with his wife and how his life has changed because of it!

Bridegroom -Example speech 1

Finally after eight and a half years, I can say this... on behalf of my wife and I, I would like to thank you all for coming, for sharing our special day with us, for your presents and your love.

I would like to thank Fred for his kind words. I know I'm supposed to be responding for my wife and I, but she's more than capable of speaking for herself, as she will prove in her own speech after mine.

I'd like to thank my Mum and Dad, Henry and Sheila, and Fred & Maggie, not only for their financial assistance, but also for their support and guidance when needed, and for leaving us to our own devices and letting us do "our own thing" when we needed to.

We'd like to show our appreciation with some flowers for each of them (flowers for mums and Maggie)

When thinking about what to put in my speech I looked at a variety of sources, but I always ended up, back with the Big Man.

The true light,

My guiding spirit,

The one who has a following of millions,

Homer Simpson.

When asked what marriage is like he responded;

"Marriage is like being married to your best friend, and he lets you play with his boobs".

Every one who knows me well will understand exactly where Homer and I, are coming from with that one.

I then considered writing a poem for today, describing all the loves of my life, so everybody would know how truly happy I am, but unfortunately I couldn't get Sophie, Harlequins, Guinness and Lardy Cake to rhyme !

Then during the research for this speech I came across a short verse written by Wilfred A Peterson called "The Art of Marriage".

I would like to read this now to Sophie, but I feel the sentiments apply equally to us all.

The Art of Marriage

A good marriage must be created,

In the art of marriage the little things, are the big things.

It is never being too old to hold hands,

It is remembering to say, "I love you", at least once each day,

It is never going to sleep angry,

It is having a mutual sense of values and common objectives,

It is standing together, facing the world,

It is forming a circle of love that gathers in the whole family,

It is speaking words of appreciation and demonstrating gratitude in thoughtful ways

It is having the capacity to forgive and forget,

It is giving each other an atmosphere, in which each can grow,

It is finding room for the things of the spirit,

It is common search for the good and the beautiful,

It is not only marrying the right partner,

It is being the right partner.

Sophie, in front of all our friends and family I promise I will try my best to practice this art.

So to my new wife, it doesn't seem five minutes since I was proposing to you on the beach, under the stars, proposing twice to you as it happens, as you made me do it again, "because it was over too fast the first time".

I'm so happy to be married to this beautiful, stunning, good looking and talented woman. I suppose every groom thinks his bride is the most beautiful in the world, and today that's how I feel.

I'm completely overwhelmed at how fantastic she looks, and feel hugely privileged that's she chosen to be my wife. I have been completely misled by the girls as to what Sophie would look like today, so much so, that she looks a million times more lovely than I could possibly have imagined.

Thank you for making this the best day of my life so far, and I hope that every day will be as happy as today.......just less expensive.

Sophie has promised not to change after we are married. So I'm looking for to more tact, more diplomacy, and many, many more made up songs around the house.

When I finally got round to telling Sophie what I do for a living, I was rather surprised to learn that not only did she knew what a quantity surveyor was and what I do for a living, but also that her Dad and Granddad were ones as well, and not just QS's but Partners in their own firm! The first meeting with Ian was a tad daunting for a newly qualified surveyor and boyfriend to say the least!

I'd also like to thank Claris, Katie and Jonathon for delivering the readings so eloquently, and to David for videoing the ceremony and these speeches.

I'm quite a superstitious sort of bloke, and I've noticed over the last week or two some very good omens for this day and for this marriage. Last week I saw a shooting star and made a wish, last Monday I saw a double rainbow, today Southampton are above Portsmouth in the football league and to cap it all Harlequins beat London Irish today and are still unbeaten and at the top of the Rugby Premiership !

Now to the "Al's", Alistair's and Alan. Thank you both for organising the stag do, which I'm told I enjoyed enormously.

Thanks to Alistair for ushing and for being my mate, it is very much appreciated (Alistair's present).

I've known Alan since we started college together some nineteen years ago, we've had some very good times together which I'm sure he'll tell you about shortly, if he can actually remember them. I'd sincerely like to thank him for being my best man today. (Alan's presents)

I should perhaps just mention that Alan suffers from a rare medical condition, which, makes him prone to embellishment and suffer delusions about fairies. He often invents the most fanciful stories, which he sincerely believes to be true. I hope you bear this in mind when he stands up to speak after Sophie.

Sophie and I would like to thank the three bridesmaids, Susan, Katy and Lauren. You've all been terrific and done a great job today and over the last few months. I'm sure you'll all agree that they all look beautiful. We'd like you to except these gifts as a token of our appreciation and as a reminder of your involvement today (presents)

And finally a toast to our three lovely, helpful, and very patient bridesmaids,

The Groom's Wedding Toast

Traditionally the shortest of the three main speeches, the Groom's wedding speech should always be concluded by the raising of a toast to the bridesmaids.

As with the Father of the Bride toast there are no set guidelines or rules, but it is advised that any Groom's wedding toast doesn't look to place too much emphasis on how beautiful the bridesmaids all look, just in case his new wife decides to take offence!

The following is a short example of a Groom's wedding toast:

"May I take this opportunity to thank each and every one of the Bridesmaids here today. You've been a great help to my new wife and I and we are both very appreciative for all your efforts.

So if everyone could please join with me and lift up their glasses and raise a toast - to our bridesmaids."

Ladies & gentlemen...the bridesmaids

Bridegroom-Example speech 2

I had a fantastic speech all worked out today but now I'm married my new wife has told me what to say

So Ladies and Gentleman I'd like to thank each and every one of you for the amount of effort you have made to be here to celebrate our marriage. We know many of you have travelled a long way to be here to celebrate with us so we hope that the night is enjoyable for you as it is special to us. you should see some disposable cameras on the tables, please feel free to use them and take pictures tough out the day

On a personal note I would especially like to thank my new in-laws Sharon and James who have done everything to make me feel welcome since I first started dating Lorraine 6 ½ years ago, in fact the whole family has. Sue, I would like to thank you for the effort you have put in making all the invitations and place cards and James I'd like to thank you for giving away Lorraine this morning so willingly, a bit to willingly if you ask me.

cue gifts and flowers

I can't stand up here without giving a special thanks to my mum who has always been there for me with support and guidance in every big decision I have made in my life, you have always been there and I cant thank you enough so here is a little token of my appreciation

cue flowers and gift

I'd also like to thank my dad for giving me guidance and pushing me towards getting a career in the RAF because if he didn't I wouldn't of joined and met Lorraine so thank you.

When I proposed to Lorraine, I put a lot of thought into what makes a good marriage. The dictionary says that a marriage is the institution whereby men and woman are joined in a special kind of social and legal dependency for the purpose of founding and maintaining a family, if only things were that simple. I've asked around and some people say a marriage consists of 3 rings, engagement ring wedding ring and suffering, others say that its an alliance of 2 people one who never remembers birthdays and anniversaries and another who never forgets. I personally think marriage is devoting all your time and effort to make that one special person happy and indulging in the good times and being there for each other through the bad. Lorraine, when I proposed to you I took it as a commitment, a commitment to making you happy and to do what I can to be there for you in anyway I possibly can until we are grey and old.

Now speaking of grey and old I like to thank my best man, when I first set the wedding day I instantly knew who I wanted to be my best man but unfortunately he couldn't make it so I settled for Nigel instead, Nigel has done nothing but look out for my brother and I ever since we were little kids, he has always given us the best advice he can, to me he is not only the best man here today but the best man I have and will ever know.

Cue gift

So no wedding is complete without testosterone ridden ushers and a pack of bridesmaids. I'm sure you all agree that they all look beautiful, and so do the bridesmaids. I would also like you to especially take note and compliment the bridesmaids on their shoes as it took more time choosing the right style colour and heel that it did my new mother-in-law to do her hair. So if I can get all the bridesmaids and ushers to come up we would like to give you all a gift to show you our gratitude

cue gifts

Now I'm not going to stand up here all day and bore you with bad jokes, that's the best mans job. I just have one task to fulfil. As you can all agree my new wife looks absolutely fantastic and I have to quote what my mum first said to Lorraine when I introduced them "what exactly do you see in my son" well to be honest I don't know but I've written a poem about what I see in you

Lorraine in everyway possible you are my best mate, you brought the first round on our blind date.

As a poor student you had hardly a dime, I'm still waiting to see that purse open a second time.

Lorraine in everyway possible your beauty is rare, With your blue green eyes and your curly long hair. We spend hours in town finding your latest trend,

Do you know that drives me around the bend?

Lorraine in everyway possible you dance so well, You will bop away till the last order bell.

The only problem is you drag me up to join, I then bust some moves my back and my groin.

Lorraine in everyway possible you are a bit bizarre, You think I can't drive when you're not in my car. You tell me to change gear, indicate and use my wipers, Next thing you will want to put me in dippers.

Lorraine in everyway possible you really look after me, You're the first to get up if the dog needs a wee. At the weekends I can lie in for a while, Then I get a job list longer than a mile.

Lorraine in everyway possible you will be a great wife, I want to make you happy my entire life. Lorraine I love you so much with all my heart, I will stand by your side till death do us part.

So thank you all again and I now will introduce the best man.

****

The Best Mans Speech

The best man's wedding speech is usually the most eagerly awaited of all the wedding speeches. Traditionally the best man's speech is the last which gives the groom the chance to get one or two quick jokes in at the best man's expense. This can be a dangerous game as the best man can always have a couple of extra stories for his speech up his sleeve if he feels the need for revenge.

When preparing your best mans speech remember to think about your audience, find out the mix of people attending and try to weave something for everyone in to your speech. Aim for your speech to be about 5 minutes but no more than 10 minutes. You will find that your best man speech takes longer when you deliver it on the day once all the laughter and cheering is factored in.

The best man's speech will contain within it:

- Thanks to the groom for his toast to the bridesmaids
- Comments on the bridal couple, particularly the groom
- The reading of any messages from absent friends and relatives
- The toasting of the bride and groom

Best man-Example speech 1

Before I undertake the customary duty of giving Martin an uncomfortable few minutes it is part of the official duty of the best man to thank Martin on behalf of the bridesmaids, Lotty, Gemma and Claire for his kind words and for having them play a part of this really special day. I have to say they all look wonderful and have done an excellent job. Indeed they are only eclipsed by Sue herself, who, I'm sure you'll all agree, looks absolutely stunning.

It is a great privilege to be asked by Martin to be his best man. He has quite generously returned the favour that I asked of him 6 years ago, during which Martin took the opportunity to make lots of cheap jokes at my expense, so I now have the right to reply.

I suppose the first thing the best man should explain is how he knows the groom. Well, being his identical twin we first met long before we can both remember, so we are very close. There's nothing I wouldn't do for Martin, likewise there's nothing Martin wouldn't do for me, in fact we spent most of our time doing nothing for each other.

I will start at the point of our early life as toddlers.

Growing up together in those early days, I am proud to say that I was an angelic child, no trouble to anyone, but the same could not be said of Martin. He showed no respect to his elder twin brother. I became an innocent victim of his loutish behaviour. "Lloyd, flush your socks down the toilet" he used to say. And under duress I did.

But that lout grew up into the well-mannered and well-presented individual we see sitting here today. Martin has matured.

For instance I can tell you that Martin is very well read - he has after all read all 45 of the Mr Men books from cover to cover. In fact, at the age of five, whilst living in Australia, Martin had a great idea to wander off into the dense, wild outback behind our house to look for Mr Jelly, whom he had read lived in the middle of a forest. He convinced me to go with him and we got terribly lost. By the time we had found our way home, there were lots of tears. Not for the fact that he had been lost in a forest, but that Martin never found Mr Jelly's house.

On the subject of Australia, it was there that Martin began a love affair which still lasts to this day. McDonalds. Age six, we were ever so excited to make our first visit to McDonalds and the great thing about this place was the kids playground - it was like a mini-theme park - things to climb, things to slide down, things to spin around in all for the enjoyment of children who had just scoffed their face with burgers and fries. It was whilst Mum, Dad, Verity and I were sat inside the restaurant that Martin, having just stepped off the swings, appeared the other side of the window. knocking loudly so that everyone in the restaurant noticed him. My parents played along and waved back...until Martin, in full sight of everyone tucking into their lunch, brought up his fast food as quickly as it had originally gone down, all over the window pane. Suddenly my parents stopped waving and momentarily tried to pretend he wasn't theirs, although sadly as Martin's twin was sat with them at their table, they couldn't fool anyone. The waitress gave them some reassurance. "Don't worry guys, that happens here all the time."

His love of fast food however never stands in the way of his enjoyment of sport. Martin usually waits until half time to get off the sofa to ring for a pizza.

Some of you may be aware of his passion for cricket. What many of you don't know is that his interest in the sport was borne during his time at school. Martin is a modest man - well, that's what he has insisted I tell you - so his cricket achievements are little known. But I can reveal today that at school, Martin SCORED more runs than any other person in the entire cricket team - that was because he was always 12th man putting up the numbers the scoreboard at the pavilion.

After school, Martin went on to study environmental science at Kings College London. I am told by his friends many of whom are here today that Martin had a natural flair for the subject. They tell me that no matter how remote a place Martin was sent away on field trips, he could gauge and interpret the direction of the wind, the contamination of the soil and the pollution of the air to produce an accurate assessment of where the nearest local pub was to skive off to have a pint of lager and a packet of crisps.

But Martin had to fund his extra curricular activities. Being a student with far too much time on his hands and always in need of an extra few quid, Martin decided to exploit a promotional campaign at Selfridges, the famous department store on London's Oxford Street. The deal was that customers were entitled to a voucher if they purchased an item from all seven floors. Martin managed to get round the store and buy small items which came to the grand total of 37 pence. It was an all time record amongst his fellow students. Selfridges had no choice but to pay out the voucher, which Martin then redeemed for cash. What's more impressive or should I say sad is that he did this seven times in one day to walk away with a hard earned voucher. Unsurprisingly, Selfridges ended their promotional campaign rather abruptly.

Although Martin studied environmental science, I began to doubt his true commitment to the green cause when he purchased his first car after leaving university, a Volkswagen Beetle. Now, I'm not sure what year the Beetle was made, though I believe the front of the car was made in the early nineties and the rear of the car some years before. Martin spent hours in that car, usually trying to get it to start. It was the only vehicle that you wouldn't use a traditional road atlas or street map to navigate your journey. Martin's Beetle was so economically inefficient and powerless that he had to plot his routes using an ordinance survey map to make sure that his entire route was downhill. With careful planning, Martin could achieve this and the only flaw was making the return journey home by the same route.

Being Martin's older twin, by a whole five minutes, I realise Martin that you have now reached the age that I was when I started this speech and with that you will gained the maturity and wisdom that I had back then. So this is probably a good time to for me to show some respect.

Joking aside, I want to say what a privilege it is today to be your best man. I couldn't wish for a better brother and how much you mean is really impossible to put into words. The whole family is proud of you Martin, and we are all thrilled to see you marrying your beautiful bride sue today

So it now gives me immense pleasure to invite you all to stand once more and raise your glasses in a toast for Martin and Sue. We wish them well for the future. To love, life, laughter and happily ever after.

Martin and Sue.

The Best Man's Wedding Toast

The last of the wedding toasts are traditionally raised by the Best Man and he has two toasts to perform; the first in response to the Groom's toast to the bridesmaids, the second to the Bride and Groom themselves. Here are a couple of example of wedding toasts for the Best Man:

"I'm sure the everyone would agree how beautiful the bridesmaids look and I know the Bride is particularly grateful for all their help and support. So without further ado, a toast, to the bridesmaids".

"Here's to my old friend, my new friend, my best friends. Ladies and gentlemen, please join with me in raising a toast to the Bride and Groom".

Best man-Example speech 2

What can you say about a man who came from humble beginnings, a man who is now quickly rising to the very top of his profession based solely on intelligence, grit and the willpower to push on where others have fallen.

A man who is beginning to distinguish himself at the very highest level amongst his peers, and where none can say a bad word against him?

But enough about me, what I'm really here for this afternoon is to talk about Peter Stirling.

Unaccustomed to public speaking as I am I have been fairly nervous before today's speeches, however Peter was very good and took me aside to help calm me, he said if I did a really good job today and went easy on him, I could be his best man the next time he gets married as well.

pause for laugh-casually

Actually me and the boys drew straws earlier on, just because I'm standing here don't think for a minute I was the winner!

Seriously though and more importantly, I'd like to start off by congratulating the happy couple, Peter and Louise, any of us here like me who has been lucky enough to spend time in their company knows what a great couple they are together, perfectly complementing each other.

When I first met Louise my impression was of a beautiful, witty, charming, clever, friendly and thoughtful person. But she soon ruined this by agreeing to marry Peter.

Speaking of Louise, I would like to say how beautiful she looks today in that fantastic dress … Peter likes it too, as he told me in the church he thinks it will blend in very well with the rest of the kitchen. pause

Peter truly is a lucky man today. Louise is a wonderful girl, and she deserves a great husband.. Thank God you married her before she had a chance to find one!

Actually, while enjoying the service this afternoon, I couldn't help thinking that it's funny how history repeats itself. I mean 30 years ago Louise's family were sending her to bed with a dummy........ and here they are again today.

I'd also like to echo Peter's earlier comments and thank everyone on their behalf for coming, sharing and witnessing their marriage day, particularly those of you that have travelled long distances, I know how hard it is to get day release! pause

I can only guess how nervous the bride and groom felt this morning, but I can assure you that this isn't the first time today I've risen from a warm seat holding a piece of paper in my hand.

Having been told the official news that I was to be Peter's best man I went ahead and purchased a book, in fact I actually got about three after panic buying in Waterstone's, the one I decided would be my bible for the event was called "the duties of the best man."

Unfortunately, I got through just a few pages and wasn't too sure if it was the best choice after reading the following and I quote:

"At the reception the best man should help keep things running smoothly by offering around drinks and introducing people".

So according to this, I should be buying you all drinks and acting as some form of high class pimp!.... so you can see why I gave up on that one!

Regrettably I never did pick it up again until last night and even then I only started flicking through a couple more pages. It has a list of do's and don'ts for the speech, which rather narrowed down my options.

Don't mention ex-girlfriends <throw away card>

Don't swear <throw away card>

Don't tell risqué jokes <throw away card>

Don't tell lies <throw away 3 cards>

Do tell mostly positive stories about the groom throw away 5 cards

So where do I start with Peter? Well for starters he's

(read intently off of paper)

Handsome

Witty

Intelligent

He's Char... Charm.... Sorry Peter .... I'm having trouble reading your handwriting on this note you gave me, you can tell me the rest later.

Another of my duty's is to make sure that certain people are thanked for their part in today, so I'd like to take some time to thank a few people who on the face of it have a fairly easy day, they have to cope with all the difficulties of standing around pouting and looking pretty, they've spent a lot of time on their hair and make up and outfits, and without them the day just wouldn't be Louise's – ladies and gentlemen, I give you the ushers - Jamie, Ross, Mark, Roscoe and Chris.

But seriously Peter, the lads here have asked me to thank you on their behalf for what is undoubtedly a great honour to be an usher, and in particular for at last getting to live out their lifelong dreams by getting to dress up like Laurence Llewellyn Bowen in public!

At this point its also customary for me to thank the groom on behalf of the bridesmaids Katie, Emma, Thea and Sophie, so with that I'd like to thank Andrew for his kind words and generous gifts.

They completed their main job admirably, which was getting Louise here on time - no mean feat as I understand she put up quite a struggle. pause

On a personal note I'd also like to thank the bridesmaids all of whom look radiant I think we'd all agree, in fact one of Peter's ushers Mark has told me if you'd all meet him later on in his room he'll thank you all personally.

I've also overheard them arguing all day about which one of them was to have the pleasure of being the first to dance with me. All I can say is ..... look, one of you has to!!

I'd also like to congratulate Peter, who has made a truly heroic attempt to cut back on his eating and drinking to get into shape for today, and personally I think he's succeeded! ....Well.... round is kind of a shape isn't it?!

I was having a quiet drink with Peter the other night and asked him what it was he wanted from his marriage, he said, "well, I want to be a model husband and I want to be a model citizen."

And he added with a cheeky grin that he also wanted to be a model lover!!

Being the naïve chap that I am, I looked up "model" in the dictionary. It said:

"a small, miniature replica of the real thing"!!!

I thought it best to ask around to see what some of Peter's friends and family would say about him: His colleagues at the Royal Bank of Scotland describe him as a first class banker – although I may have misheard them.

-some other words you could use to describe Peter are: charming, urbane, intelligent, and entertaining…but nobody said those, so I won't use them.

He was once described as arrogant, conceited, insensitive and selfish...and let's face it, if anyone would know him, it would be his mum.

Speaking of his mum, and dad for that matter, Jenny and Kerr have informed me that the day that changed their life was the 3rd of February, 1972.......You see that day Jenny had a small win on the pools...........No, that was the day young Peter was born, 8 pounds and 7 ounces, 12 full hours in labour, complete and utter agony for his mother, and nothing much has changed since.

Apparently the young Peter took a keen interest in sex and booze from a very early age. When he was three years old his curiosity about alcohol got the better of him and he managed to tip over a 1 gallon jar of homemade elderberry wine off of the shelf onto the brand new carpet.

When he was four, he was with his mother in a doctors surgery staring at a family planning poster of a pregnant woman, and was heard to say in a loud voice:

"baby grows in mummy's tummy. But nobody knows how it goes from the daddy to the mummy, do they mummy." Which reminds me of my last duty as best man. addressing Peter "Peter, before your wedding night we need to have a little chat after about mummies and daddies!"

It wouldn't be too far off the mark to say that I could shovel more dirt on the gentleman seated to my left / right than a Taliban Cave digger.

Now as you might have guessed there are plenty of stories that I could tell about Peter, but I couldn't actually think of one that would be appropriate. When I say appropriate, I mean one that would have him squirming in his seat and sweating more than Pavarotti on a treadmill.

However after much deliberation I managed to recall one or two.

I first met Peter at King Edwards School in Bath when we were both 16 and entering the lower sixth to study for our A levels.

I sat next to him in our first class together where he produced onto his desk a brand new black leather executive brief case. Upon opening said case it revealed its contents.....nothing except a single pair of black gentleman's socks, when I quizzed him why he gave me a wry smile and lifted up his trouser legs, to reveal himself sporting a truly garish pair of bright red socks!

Apparently he was afraid of being asked to remove the red socks and the posh briefcase was only to carry round a spare pair!

Andrew was known amongst his friends when younger as the "magpie" due to his wild eye for fashion.

Once when a lot of us had gone out to a nightclub he managed to distinguish himself by being the only person there to feel the need to wear skiing goggles all night long.

Another night out in Bath myself and Ross went to meet him before going out for a quiet drink, we had dressed quite casually in jeans, t shirts, dark jackets and shoes,

However Peter clearly had some bigger and more important fashion agenda to adhere to, as he appeared in a pink, white and red silk shirt covered in a rose motif, an exceptionally bright green ankle length woollen coat with large golden bones instead of buttons, his trousers tucked into German army 15 hole boots and atop his head a top hat at a rather jaunty angle!...........

To this day he thinks the reason we were refused entry into pubs was because we looked too young!

Thankfully as the years passed he stopped dressing like the 1970's love child of Liberace and Sir Elton John, but his occasional wild ape man like urges still haunted him.

Not so many years ago Peter was enjoying a quiet get together with some old and close friends, but soon decided things were too quiet for a man of his refined tastes.

He soon left the party under a dark cloud leaving behind him a terrible trail of ripped out telephone cords, smashed mirrors and deeply offended friends, yet this was merely the beginning of his long dark night!

Hailing a taxi our hero headed home to west London. Upon arriving at his doorstep he pulled the old Scottish trick of discovering he had no money on him. So offered to write the cabbie a cheque.

Because of Peter's extremely advanced state of refreshment, even after several minutes of determined scribbling he couldn't manage to write his own name on the cheque book.

At this point the driver lost all patience with him and drove Peter around the corner to Ladbroke Grove police station.

The police had more luck and were able to coax his unsteady hand down onto the cheque book just long enough to produce some sort of acceptable squiggle. Then all was well with the world once more.......Until.........

Peter walked outside the station to find the taxi driver had driven off and left him stranded a few miles from his door in the early hours of the morning.

Peter decided then that as he had just paid the taxi man to take him home, a massive miscarriage of justice had unfolded on the scales of the Guildford four or the Birmingham six. He decided the sensible thing to do was to go back into the station and inform the constables of how wrong they had been.

A heated debate between himself and the desk Sergeant soon started. As the words flowed back and forth across the desk Peter became more and more enraged, the red ape-man like mist was slowly descending.

To prevent this gross miscarriage of justice from continuing, Peter decided the best course of action was to launch himself across the desk with all fists flying right at the sergeant, screaming the immortal words "you'll never take me alive copper".

Well in the end six policemen did manage to take Peter alive, as they restrained him and put him into the back of a waiting black Mariah, and then drove him down the road to the cells at Shepherds Bush police station where he was locked up for the night.

An extremely humbled Peter was released the next morning without charge, he took the long and lonely walk home to think about his misdemeanours, and thankfully this proved to be the end of his short, savage but quite glorious career with the police.

I would now like to share with you all a conversation I overheard while in the chemists last week between a father and a son. The boy was quizzing his dad as to why condoms are available in 3 packs, 6 packs and 12 packs.

"Well son, teenage boys buy the 3 packs as they use 1 on a Friday night, 1 on a Saturday night and 1 on a Sunday night."

He then says young guys in their 20's buy the 6 packs as they use 2 on a Friday night, 2 on a Saturday night and 2 on a Sunday night.

So the boy says "well who uses the 12 packs then dad?" "Ahhh the hallowed 12 packs" he says, "The 12 packs are used by married men, as they use 1 in January, 1 in February, 1 in March" etc...

And in light of this we would like to help Andy on his way by presenting him with the married man starter pack. Jamie, if could you do the honours please? Presents a 12 pack of condoms.

It was our intention to give you the 6 pack, but we couldn't deny you sex for six months of the year.

Advice

I've got some words of advice on marriage for you here Peter:

Someone once said that marriage is a 50/50 partnership, but anyone who believes that clearly knows nothing about women or fractions!

To help the course of true love run smoothly never forget those three very important words you must say every day....... "you are right dear."

Also it is very important to get on with your mother in law, a friend of mine hasn't spoken to his in two years, not because he doesn't like her, he just doesn't like to interrupt her!

Also a small piece of advice on marriage for you too Louise-

Don't keep him in the dog house too long, or he might give his bone to the woman next door!

So now we just have a couple of telegrams:

1. Dear Peter, congratulations on getting married and winning our big spender of the month award! From all the girls at central chambers exotic dancing club.

2. Dear Peter, hope you have made the right decision, I`ll always remember the long, lovely evenings we spent around my swimming pool, all my love, Michael Barrymore.

And finally there seems to be a bit of confusion over where Peter and Louise are going on their honeymoon, I thought, perhaps like many of you here that they were off to California, but now I'm not so sure.

After speaking to Peter earlier today I think they're going to North Wales ....Or at least I think that's what he meant when he said he was going to Bangor all week!

Toast

I'd like to finish up by saying what a great honour it's been to be Peter's best man today, and I'm glad he's finally admitted that I am the better man!

We've been firm friends for fifteen years now, in which time we've hardly argued, and often shared our dark sense of humour together, much to the consternation of our girlfriends. You've been a true friend to me Peter, and I look forward to knowing you and Louise for the rest of our lives!

So then, Ladies and Gentleman, it gives me immense pleasure, not to mention immense relief, to invite you all to be upstanding and raise your glasses in a toast to Peter and Louise, we wish them well for the future, and may they enjoy a long and happy marriage.

So may I be the first to give you the new "Mr and Mrs Stirling

****

Brides Speech

Nowadays more Brides are keen to say a few words on their special day. It is here you can thank your guests for coming and say a special thank you to your wedding entourage. Without your family and friends, your day wouldn't have been the same.

In your wedding speech you may want to acknowledge special friends and remember loved ones who aren't there with you on the day.

You can dedicate part of your Bride speech to thanking your parents for their support and for everything you have been through with them so far. You can include some special moments that you have shared with them that you hold dear to your heart and will cherish forever.

In your Bride speech you will want to say a special something to your new husband; maybe a special memory that have when you first met, what was about him that made you fall in love with him and to tell him your looking forward to the years ahead with him. Give him the recognition he deserves.

Brides speech-Example speech 1

You may well be wondering what the Bride is doing making a speech. Well, those of you who know me well know that I always have talked a lot (& loudly!) and usually find a way to get my two penneth worth in so it probably is no surprise! I also wanted to say thank you to those deserving in my own words.

I feel privileged to be sharing our day with most of the friends and family who have been important to us during our lives. Many of you have travelled from a far :- America, Ireland, Switzerland, Spain and even Wales & Yorkshire to be here.

Thanks to all of you for the efforts and sacrifices you have made to be with us today.

To Carol and John, thank you for making me feel so welcome in the Hearst family. Thank you for raising Steve so well, although I understand that the warranty is out of date now and the refund deadline has long since passed. I might keep him for a while though as he has so many qualities, charm, brains and beauty are sadly the only ones missing.... and thank you also for the generous financial contribution that meant we could have a honeymoon we really wanted.

Mum - thank you for your love, support and care over the last 29 years and also for your contributions to making this such a special day.

Steve, thank you for biting the bullet, proposing and turning up today, on time and appropriately dressed. You are the love of my life, my best friend and now my husband. I don't think anybody could be happier than I am today, and I can't wait for us to share the rest of our lives together. It means a lot to be your wife & I'm sure you're happy now that you can start to let yourself go

Finally, I have some small gifts for my beautiful bridesmaids - Kath, Liz and Corinne. It's been wonderful having you all here today - I'm sure your presence has enhanced the photos no end! But seriously - thank you.

And now, I'd like you all to stand and raise your glasses in a toast to the bridesmaids......

Brides toast

Traditionally the bride did not make a speech, so there is no formal toast for her to make. This means she can choose to toast whoever she likes. Popular choices are her parents/groom's parents and family, her bridesmaids/helpers, absent friends, particularly if one is a parent, or close relative, and/or her new husband!

Brides Speech-Example 2

Did anyone see that polar bear walk by just now? No? Shame, they make such terrific icebreakers.

I know it's not really traditional for a bride to make a speech at her wedding, let alone before the groom but anyone who knows me knows how hard it can be to keep me quiet and today is no exception. However, I promise to try and keep it short as I know the day is full of speeches and I'm also quite keen to see my Dad on the dance floor.

Before I start I would just like to say - me in a dress!!! Take a long hard look and remember this moment guys, it's a one off! I never thought I'd find myself here with N today as I'd always hoped for an arranged marriage. Turns out George Clooney wasn't so keen though so........

All kidding aside thank-you to all of you for coming here today to share our day with us. I know for the majority of you it has meant making huge efforts in rearranging your personal lives as well as arranging travel and accommodation and we appreciate that more than you realise. Of course there are some people and some faces missing as I look around today who, for various reasons, cannot be with us to share the day. I'd like to make a toast to these people who are far away today but still in our thoughts, or looking down on us, hopefully with a wee dram of their own. So would you all please raise your glasses for a moment to "Absent friends and loved ones".

I'd also like to thank some very special people while I am up here.

Mum. There just are not words to say how much I owe to you or how much I love you. If anyone has ever epitomised the phrase "my rock" it's you. You have always been my role model, my confidante and my biggest fan. Over the years you have given me a combination of love support and sound advice coupled with free rein to go and make a total muppet of myself, which I frequently did.

And my Dad's. Most people stand and say how lucky they are to have a wonderful father. I am truly blessed for I have two men to call my Dad. You are both very different men yet you both offer me unconditional love and support, and always have. Without both of you I would not be where I am today and I was very proud and honoured to have two such special men by my side as I walked down the aisle earlier.

Today I also gain another set of parents: M&S. From the day I met you I felt welcomed and accepted. I am very lucky to have such great in-laws. Thank-you for raising N so well and rest assured I will look after and love him just as well. Am I right in thinking there's no warranty card for him? No? Worth a thought. I have a small gift here for you from me to say thank-you for welcoming me into your family.

And our wedding party. I know N has some gifts to give out yet too and some thank-you's of his own but I would like to take time to thank my bridesmaids. K, my chief bridesmaid is also my best friend, though she does like to confuse the new doctors at work by introducing herself to them as my life partner. Sorry N! She has been a true friend to me in the last year listening to both tears and hysterical laughter - often together, and is one in a million. Thanks K. I hope this goes some way to making up for the Bridezilla act.

And my two other bridesmaids - my baby sisters. You are both beautiful, amazing people and I am more proud of you than you know. Telling M her dress was lime green with purple daisies on it made for good sport for Mum and I at the time but I think you will all agree they look stunning - not really allowed on my day but I'll forgive you! These are for you.

Lastly onto the reason I am stood here dressed like a girl for the first and hopefully last time. N, well I did tell you all you had to do today was shave and turn up. You did and babe you look amazing. I don't think I have ever loved you more. We chose Chasing Cars for our wedding music as its "our song" and the words have always said how we feel about each other. I'd like to reiterate a few of those words to you now. "I don't know where, confused about how as well. Just know that these things will never change for us at all". People often say if you can't marry the one you live with, marry the one you can't live without. I've done both. We don't always make life easy for each other but you are my soul mate and I would never have it any other way.

With that I would like to let you all breathe a huge sigh of relief that I am going to shut the heck up, and turn you over to my husband, possibly the only time her can ever have the last word without it being "yes dear you're right". Over to you babe.

****

Maid of Honour

Speeches are not just for the men of the wedding party. Nowadays many ladies in the entourage like to say a few words and this is a great way to say a special thank you to the couple for asking you to play an important role on their special day.

The Maid of Honour speech should be light-hearted and have just the right amount of sentiment to allow for some oohs and aaahs! The guests will love to hear some funny stories about the bride; maybe some anecdotes of when you grew up together or a special milestone that you both shared. Try to include poignant message; say something from the heart. This is a great time for you to tell the Bride how much she means to you!

You can include in your Maid of Honour speech a special note about the Bride's parents and maybe a happy memory if you have a relationship with them.

In the Maid of Honour speech, you should thank the other Bridesmaids for their help in making today wonderful for their friend and for being a big part of the special day. You should also compliment the ushers, finally proposing a toast.

Maid of Honour -Example speech1

For those of you that don't already know me I'm Rebecca, Xanthe's 'slightly' older sister.

When Xanthe first asked me to give her away I felt two things, the first was one of extreme and enormous pride that she'd asked me, and the second was 'Oh my God' I have to do a speech. So please don't worry this won't take too long.

I would like to thank the vicar for a lovely service, the vicars mate for keeping an eye out on the weather, although Uncle Anthony could well have had something to do with that and Victoria, Xanthe's lifelong friend and beautiful bridesmaid. I am also delighted to have my Mum, sisters and brother here today to celebrate Xanthe's (and Stuarts) day, one which I hope is the start of many more 'happiest days of their life'.

Xanthe has given me, and all of my family some incredibly happy and joyous moments over the years. She was a delight to grow up with, and has always provided us with some memorable moments.

Having known Xanthe all her life I have a huge library of stories to leave her embarrassed and humiliated, but out of respect for her on her big day I have decided NOT to tell them...

So I'm not going to tell to tell you about the milkman, yes they were around in those days, asking me how my brother was on many an occasion – well done Mum, Xanthe always loved that hair cut,

And I'm not going to admit that I did my bit towards Xanthe's hairstyles when I cut her fringe to about 1cm and it took most of the next 5 years to grow back. In fact I'm surprised she ever forgave me! I can so clearly remember the horror on her face when I finally let her see it

And I'm not going to mention the fact that Xanthe as a young child was at her happiest playing on her own with her fisher price toys, she liked the red headed one with the long fringe best!! – Funny that!

Xanthe, as I'm sure you all know is fiercely independent – I am reminded of a particular suitcase, small red one, that was often packed on her way to leave home for one shore or another, and this one's first outing was to go back to Yorkshire with my Uncle George, even then an old man when she was about 4 years old. As far as I can recall the only things she'd actually packed were books – and perhaps that little Fisher Price friend? When Xanthe first introduced Stuart to us all, well we weren't quite sure what to make of him really, and I'm sure Stuart felt exactly the same, I think someone coming into a family of four sisters and a brother can find the whole experience quite daunting but Stuart took it all in his stride and has since become the comedian and magician of family social events...............

ON a more serious note, I hope you all agree that the wedding so far, has been a huge success, I would like to thank all of you for celebrating the day with us especially those who have travelled almost the length of the country to be here.

It has been an absolute honour for me, Xanthe, to give you away today; you are a fantastic sister, great daughter and brilliant friend.

I've never seen you happier than you have been over these last few years with Stuart; I hope the best for you now and always

Finally, On behalf of my Mum, my sisters and brother, and of course all our partners, not forgetting Zach and Maddy, I would like to welcome Stuart, his Mum and Dad, Jill and Roy, and his brother, Pete, into our family, we all look forward to getting to know you better.

Now ladies and gentleman, it gives me great pleasure to invite you all to stand and raise your glasses in a toast to the bride and groom, Xanthe and Stuart. To love, laughter and happily ever after – Cheers!

Maid of honour-Example speech 2

Good afternoon, Ladies & Gentlemen – My name is Alison and I am Richard, the groom's wonderful older sister!

On behalf of the Bridesmaids & Ushers I would like to thank the Bride & Groom

It has been a wonderful day so far and well done to Zena with a little bit of help from Richard for organising it so well

I am very proud, and honoured, to be here today as "best woman" to my little brother Richard.

I am doing this today on behalf of the REAL "Best Man", our brother Gary, who sadly, as many of you are aware is not here with us today, though if Gary has anything to do with it he is here in Spirit.

He would have been absolutely delighted for Richard & Zena and would also have been checking out the ladies......

Can we make sure our glasses are full and just take a moment to stand and raise our glasses in a toast to the real best man ..... To Gary

****

8

POEMS FOR THE WEDDING

Having sampled a few essential speeches, which cover the whole range of a wedding, below is a sample of Classic Poems which can be used within the context of a wedding, either preceding or following the speeches. Poems are not everyone's cup of tea but some brave souls like to incorporate either own or someone else's poem. Those laid out below are well-known classic poems and can freely be used. All you need to do is to find one to suit.

Power Of Love
By Hemakumar Nanayakkara

Drown deeply in starry sparkling eyes
Bathe soothingly in the sea of romance
Float smoothly on curving water waves
Disappear the blues in aquamarine ocean.

Fly high across unlimited moonlit sky
Stray among stars in a faraway milky way
Glide towards galaxies of celestial lights
Let the troubles disappear in afar darkness.

Blissful whispers flow all over in the air
Moments of joy adorn the serenity of lives
Wondrous times harmonize every heart and mind
Existence of true love lasts forever-timeless.

Swiftly lead into raptures over divine true romance
Adorable smiles blooming like blossoms of red roses
Trail bewitching paths cherishing every amorous moment
United hearts surrender to the supreme power of love.

You are my description of love
You are my description of friend
You are my description of everything
You are my description of beginning to end.

You have put me on a pedestal
You make me feel ten feet tall
You've always been there for me
You've loved me through it all.

You've stood by me through thick and thin
You've always been patient and kind
Just thought I'd let you know
You're the owner of this heart of mine.

So you ask how long I'll love you
Well this is what I have to say
Past, present, future, always
Forever and a day!

"She Walks in Beauty" by Lord Byron

She walks in beauty, like the night
Of cloudless climes and starry skies;
And all that's best of dark and bright
Meet in her aspect and her eyes:
Thus mellow'd to that tender light

Which heaven to gaudy day denies.

One shade the more, one ray the less,
Had half impair'd the nameless grace
Which waves in every raven tress,
Or softly lightens o'er her face;
Where thoughts serenely sweet express
How pure, how dear their dwelling-place.

And on that cheek, and o'er that brow,
So soft, so calm, yet eloquent,
The smiles that win, the tints that glow,
But tell of days in goodness spent,
A mind at peace with all below,
A heart whose love is innocent!

"Roads Go Ever Ever On" By J.R.R Tolkien

Roads go ever ever on,
Over rock and under tree,
By caves where never sun has shone,
By streams that never find the sea;
Over snow by winter sown,
And through the merry flowers of June,
Over grass and over stone,
And under mountains in the moon.
Roads go ever ever on
Under cloud and under star,
Yet feet that wandering have gone
Turn at last to home afar.
Eyes that fire and sword have seen
And horror in the halls of stone

Look at last on meadows green
And trees and hills they long have known.

"To Be One With Each Other" by George Eliot

What greater thing is there for two human souls
than to feel that they are joined together to strengthen
each other in all labor, to minister to each other in all sorrow,
to share with each other in all gladness,
to be one with each other in the
silent unspoken memories?

"A White Rose" by JB O'Reilly

The red rose whispers of passion,
And the white rose breathes of love;
O, the red rose is a falcon,
And the white rose is a dove.
But I send you a cream-white rosebud
With a flush on its petal tips;
For the love that is purest and sweetest
Has a kiss of desire on the lips

"Love Is A Great Thing" by Thomas à Kempis

Love is a great thing, yea, a great and thorough good. By itself it
makes that is heavy light; and it bears evenly all that is uneven.

It carries a burden which is no burden; it will not be kept back by
anything low and mean; it desires to be free from all wordly
affections, and not to be entangled by any outward prosperity, or
by any adversity subdued.

Love feels no burden, thinks nothing of trouble, attempts what is above its strength, pleads no excuse of impossibility. It is therefore able to undertake all things, and it completes many things, and warrants them to take effect, where he who does not love would faint and lie down.

Though weary, it is not tired; though pressed it is not straitened; though alarmed, it is not confounded; but as a living flame it forces itself upwards and securely passes through all.

Love is active and sincere, courageous, patient, faithful, prudent and manly.

"Hope is the Thing with Feathers" by Emily Dickinson

Hope is the thing with feathers
That perches in the soul,
And sings the tune without the words,
And never stops at all,

And sweetest in the gale is heard;
And sore must be the storm
That could abash the little bird
That kept so many warm.

I've heard it in the chilliest land,
And on the strangest sea;
Yet, never, in extremity
It asked a crumb of me.

"Touched by an Angel" by Maya Angelou

We, unaccustomed to courage
exiles from delight
live coiled in shells of loneliness
until love leaves its high holy temple
and comes into our sight
to liberate us into life.

Love arrives
and in its train come ecstasies
old memories of pleasure
ancient histories of pain.
Yet if we are bold,
love strikes away the chains of fear
from our souls.

We are weaned from our timidity
In the flush of love's light
we dare be brave
And suddenly we see
that love costs all we are
and will ever be.
Yet it is only love
which sets us free.

"I Love You" by Roy Croft

I love you
Not only for who you are
But for what I am when I am with you.
I love you

Not only for what you have made of yourself
But for what you are making of me.
I love you for the part of me that you bring out.
I love you for putting your hand into my heart
And passing over all the foolish, weak things that you can't help.
Dimly seeing there and drawing out, into the light all the
beautiful belongings
That no one else had looked quite far enough to find.
You have done it without a touch, without a word, without a
sign.

"La Reina" (The Queen) by Pablo Neruda

I have named you queen.

There are taller than you, taller.
There are purer than you, purer.
There are lovelier than you, lovelier.
But you are the queen.

When you go through the streets
No one recognizes you.
No one sees your crystal crown, no one looks
At the carpet of red gold
That you tread as you pass,
The nonexistent carpet.

And when you appear
All the rivers sound
In my body, bells
Shake the sky,
And a hymn fills the world.

Only you and I,
Only you and I, my love,
Listen to me.

"To Love is Not to Possess" by James Kavanaugh

To love is not to possess,
To own or imprison,
Nor to lose one's self in another.
Love is to join and separate,
To walk alone and together,
To find a laughing freedom
That lonely isolation does not permit.
It is finally to be able
To be who we really are
No longer clinging in childish dependency
Nor docilely living separate lives in silence,
It is to be perfectly one's self
And perfectly joined in permanent commitment
To another--and to one's inner self.
Love only endures when it moves like waves,
Receding and returning gently or passionately,
Or moving lovingly like the tide
In the moon's own predictable harmony,
Because finally, despite a child's scars
Or an adult's deepest wounds,
They are openly free to be
Who they really are--and always secretly were,
In the very core of their being
Where true and lasting love can alone abide.

9

CLASSIC QUOTES FOR THE WEDDING

Below are some examples of famous quotes which can be used as a part of any wedding speech. You can pick one or two out that you might want to use in order to embellish your speech.

....

Love looks not with the eyes, but with the mind
~ William Shakespeare ~

Better to have loved and lost, than to have never loved at all
~ St. Augustine~

A part of you has grown in me. And so you see, it's you and me together forever and never apart, maybe in distance, but never in heart.
~ Author Unknown ~

My first glance fell on your heart
~ Johann F.C. Schiller ~

Love gives naught but itself and takes naught but from itself. Love possesses not nor would it be possessed; for love is sufficient unto love.
~ Kahlil Gibran ~

Within you I lose myself
Without you I find myself
Wanting to be lost again.
~ Unknown ~

There is only one happiness in life,
to love and be loved.
~ George Sands ~

My beloved is mine and I am his
~ Song of Songs ~

Whatever our souls are made up, his and mine are the same
~ Emily Bronte ~

Come live with me, and be my love,
And we will some new pleasures prove
Of golden sands, and crystal brooks,
With silken lines, and silver hooks
~ John Donne ~

Soulmates
two halves of the same soul
joining together in lifes journey
~ Author Unknown ~

You don't marry someone you can live with - you marry the
person who you cannot live without
~ Author Unknown ~

Spread love everywhere you go: first of all in your own house.
Give love to your children, to your wife or husband, to a next

door neighbor... Let no one ever come to you without leaving better and happier. Be the living expression of God's kindness; kindness in your face, kindness in your eyes, kindness in your smile, kindness in your warm greeting.
~ Mother Theresa ~

Tis better to have loved and lost
than to never have loved at all
~ Alfred, Lord Tennyson ~

If I could reach up and hold a star for every time you've made me smile, the entire evening sky would be in the palm of my hand
~ Author Unknown ~

There is no remedy for love than to love more
~ Henry David Thoreau ~

You are always new,
The last of your kisses was ever the sweetest.
~ John Keats ~

Love is a smoke raised by the fume of sighs.
~ William Shakespeare ~

Marriage is the golden ring in a chain whose
beginning is a glance and whose ending is Eternity.
~ Kahlil Gibran ~

How sweet a thing it is to love---
And to be loved again.
~ Henry Howard Brownell ~

Love gives naught but itself and takes naught but
from itself. Love possesses not nor would it be
possessed; for love is sufficient unto love.
~ Kahlil Gibran ~

If I could reach up and hold a star for every time you've made me
smile, the entire evening sky would be in the palm of my hand.
~ Author Unknown ~

It's not my ear you whispered into, but my heart. It's not my lips
that you kissed, but my soul.
~ Author Unknown ~

Love can touch us one time
and last for a lifetime,
and never let go till we're gone.
~ Theme from the movie "Titanic" ~

Being deeply loved by someone gives you strength while loving
someone deeply gives you courage.
~ Tzo, Lao ~

You call it madness, but I call it love.
~ Don Byas ~

Sympathy constitutes friendship; but in love there is a sort of
antipathy, or opposing passion. Each strives to be the other, and
both together make up one whole.
~ Samuel Taylor Coleridge ~

Look, lovers: almost separately they come
towards us through the flowery grass and slowly;

parting's so far from thought of, they indulge
the extravagance of walking unembraced.
~ Ranier Maria Rilke ~

It is the man and woman united that makes the complete human
being. Separate she lacks his force of body and strength of reason;
he her softness, sensibility and acute discernment. Together they
are most likely to succeed in the world.
~ Benjamin Franklin ~

Love does not consist of gazing at each other,
but looking outward in the same direction.
~ Antoine de Saint-Exupery ~

There are only four questions of value in life, Don Octavio.
What is sacred?
Of what is the spirit made?
What is worth living for?
What is worth dying for?
The answer to each is the same:
Only love.
~ From the movie "Don Juan DeMarco" ~

Love is the joy of the good,
the wonder of the wise,
the amazement of the Gods.
~ Plato ~

Now join your hands, and with your hands your hearts.
~ William Shakespeare ~

Give all to love
~ Waldo Ralph Emerson ~

We two have found each other... different yet alike
We have grown together in love and understanding
~ Author Unknown ~

True love is like ghosts, which everybody talks about and few
have seen.
~ Francois de La Rochefoucauld ~

Some love lasts a lifetime. True love lasts forever.
~ Author Unknown ~

Where there is love there is life.
~ Mahatma Gandhi ~

If I never met you, I would have dreamt you into being.
~ Sebastian Chantoix ~

All you need is love.
~ John Lennon ~

If love is great, and there are no greater things, then what I feel
for you must be the greatest.
~ Author Unknown ~

Grow old along with me
The best is yet to be,
The last of life, for which the first was made.
Our times are in his hand.
~ Robert Browning ~

For I have found the one whom my soul loves.
~ Song of Solomon ~

Life is the flower for which love is the honey.
~ Victor Hugo ~

Doubt thou the stars are fire
Doubt that the sun doth move
Doubt truth to be a liar
But never doubt thou love
~ William Shakespeare ~

Oh my love's like a red, red rose
That's newly sprun in June
Oh my love's like a melody
That's sweetly sung in tune
~ Robert Burns ~

We all want to fall in love. Why? Because that experience makes us feel completely alive. Where every sense is heightened, every emotion is magnified, our everyday reality is shattered and we are flying into the heavens. It may only last a moment, an hour, an afternoon. But that doesn't diminish its value. Because we are left with memories that we treasure for the rest of our lives.
~ Author Unknown ~

10

SAMPLE WEDDING JOKES

When telling jokes at a wedding, you should always keep within the bounds of good taste. The below are a few jokes which can be used before, during or after a wedding speech. For more jokes, you should look at the list of useful websites at the back of this book.

Sample jokes

"What is Marriage?"
When she was younger, my daughter was struggling to grasp the concept of marriage so I got the wedding album out and showed her the photos. "So do you understand now?" I asked her. "I think so" she said, "So this is when mummy came to work for us?".

'Husband Wanted'
Before I met my partner I tried everything I could to get a man, and even inserted a 'Husband Wanted' ad in the paper. It was quite strange really, but within a matter of hours I had tons of responses all saying the same thing, 'You Can Have Mine!'

'Revenge'
Having been married for some time now, the best piece of advice I can give you is that if ever a man comes along and tries to steal your wife the best form of revenge is to let him keep her!

'Money Troubles'

We were having an argument the other week about money and I said to my wife that if only she could learn how to cook and clean we could fire the maid. As quick as a flash she said if I could learn how to make love, we could fire the gardener, chauffeur and the butler!"

'Wedding Costs'

Just after she got engaged, my daughter asked me how much it costs to get married. I told her I wasn't sure - I was still paying!

'Marriage Cheat'

The other day I asked my wife if she'd ever cheated on me and, whilst reluctant at first she eventually admitted she had on two occasions. 'When was the first?' I asked. 'Well remember when you needed that operation on holiday but we didn't have travel insurance so couldn't afford to pay? But then out of nowhere the doctor agreed to do it for free?'. "Wow - you did that for me - I am so lucky to have you. When was the other?". 'Well, remember when you wanted to become captain of the golf club and were 23 votes short?'.....

'Definition of Marriage

Does anyone here know the definition of marriage? Well, according to the Oxford English Dictionary, and I quote, 'Marriage: The most expensive way of getting your laundry done for free.'

'Left at Airport'

A stewardess turns to a man on a plane and says, "Sorry Sir, but we appear to have left your wife behind at the airport.". "Thank goodness" says the man, "I thought I was going deaf!"

'Arranged Marriage'

A son asked his father "Is it true Dad that in Asia some men don't know their wives until they get married?". The father replies, "No son, that happens everywhere!"

'Son-In-Law'

I remember the first time I met 'X'. "So You're the man who wants to be my son-in-law?" he asked. "No" I replied. "But this is the only way I can marry your daughter!"

'The £50 Gamble'

Before today I must admit I had three women chasing after me so I decided to set them a test to help me decide which two to ditch. I gave each of them £50 to see what they'd do with the cash. The first woman bought me a brand new designer shirt, the second bought herself some sexy lingerie for us to enjoy and the third invested it wisely and brought me back £100. I thought long and hard about what each one had done, but in the end decided to go with the one with the biggest breasts!

'Love, Lust & Marriage'

For anyone who doesn't know, here are the definitions of love, lust and marriage. Love is when you only leave the house to buy flowers and chocolates. Lust is when you only leave the house to buy some sexy lingerie. Marriage is when you only leave the house when you're allowed to.

'Round for Dinner'

A few years ago I invited the Groom around for dinner and my wife flew off the handle. "Why have you invited him around? she said, "The dishes are dirty, there's no food in the house and you can think again if you want me to cook you both a nice meal". "Exactly" I said, "The poor guy's thinking of getting married!"

'How Many Kids?'

The Bride's always wanted three children, the Groom just the two. Just before the wedding, the Groom decided to put his foot down and announced that after their second child he would have a vasectomy. Without a moment of hesitation the Bride replied "That's fine, I just hope you'll love the third one as if it's your own."

****

Useful websites

Speech ideas

The websites below can give you a helping hand in getting your speech together.

www.thebestmanspeech.com
Gives loads of examples

www.public-speaking.org

This is the website of the Advanced Public Speaking Institute, with lots of articles on all aspects of speech making organised by category.

Sources of quotations
A good quotation can be invaluable in helping move your speech along and bring to its conclusion. the websites below will help you out with quotes and poems.
www.lovepoemsandquotes.com
 Verse and quotations to give your speech that extra sparkle.

www.poemsforfree.com
Provides many ready to use poems, including for the best man.

www.apoemforyou.co.uk
This site offers a personalised poem writing service.

Sources of jokes

The sites below can help with a few jokes that can be inserted in your speech if you so wish.

www.ahajokes.com
This site has hundreds of good clean jokes organised by category.

www.prestationhelper.co.uk
You should click on the best man section for a range of jokes. This site also helps with PowerPoint presentations if so wished.